# Radiant

## MORE STORIES OF
## DARING
## TEEN SAINTS

*Colleen Swaim*

Liguori
LIGUORI, MISSOURI

Imprimi Potest: Harry Grile, CSsR
Provincial, Denver Province, The Redemptorists
Published by Liguori Publications, Liguori, Missouri 63057
To order, call 800-325-9521 or visit www.liguori.org

**Library of Congress Cataloging-in-Publication Data**

Swaim, Colleen.
    Radiate : more stories of daring teen saints / Colleen Swaim.—1st ed.
    p. cm.
    1. Christian saints—Biography—Juvenile literature. 2. Catholic teenagers—Religious life—Juvenile literature. I. Title.
    BX4655.3.S935 2012
    270.092'535—dc23
                                                                        2012024595

p ISBN 978-0-7648-2147-9
e ISBN 978-0-7648-6739-2

Image credits: Shutterstock: pages 100, 105, 107; Wikipedia: pages 2, 7, 11, 14, 24, 30, 42, 45, 54, 57, 59, 64, 68 (lower), 74, 84, 104, 110, 123, 125, 126; santosybeatos.blogspot.com: page 40; Catholic Church in Korea: page 137; sources unknown: 17, 28, 46, 47, 55, 66, 68 (upper), 70, 71, 78, 87, 88, 89, 90, 104, 109, 110, 112, 122, 124, 132

Additional sources and permissions: pages 142-144

Printed in the United States of America
16 15 14 13 12  /  5 4 3 2 1

First Edition

# Contents

# Dedication

*For Zeke, who is a very good baby and*
*who was born sometime*
*in the middle of writing this book.*

2013

To: Grace with Love,
From: Mark & Sarah
Happy Birthday Sweetheart!

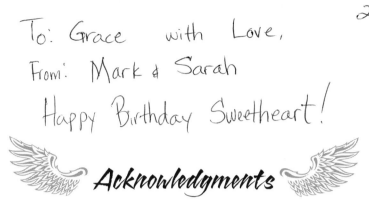

# Acknowledgments

Very special thanks go to my husband, Matt Swaim, who acted in the capacity of research assistant, awesome dad, and caffeine procurer during the time period in which I worked on this book (including, but not limited to, cloth diaper laundering, serenading with Am I a Man or a Muppet? and baby chin tickling). We are very fortunate indeed.

Additionally, I am indebted to Dan and Arica Egan and family for their faithful Zeke-sitting; Lisa Hendey for her incredible and selfless encouragement of Catholic writers and their craft; Annie Mitchell for her friendship and reflection on the pallium Mass; Camille Ng for the contribution and excellent explanation of his card trick; Brian O'Neel for his resources on the plight of Christians in North Korea; Kathy Pluth for the kind use of her translation of *Agnes beatae virginis*; and Sacred Heart Radio for the gift that is their apostolate and the generous support of *Ablaze*.

 *Foreword*

As a mom of young men, I know that sometimes efforts to talk with a teen about anything remotely religious run the risk of being met with rolled eyes, distraction, and perhaps even outward hostility. And yet tell a group of kids a story that involves a scorned suitor, a brothel, a war-torn society, otherworldly apparitions, or an untimely death under violent circumstances and you have the makings of the latest blockbuster movie they're all dying to see. Our youth today are storytellers who use new and fantastic tools to communicate their passions. They are connectors who are always looking to meet their newest friend. And yes, in their own unique and often infectious ways, they are believers in our Church: her past, her present, and her future.

With *Radiate*, my friend and fellow saint-enthusiast Colleen Swaim has given us all a gift—a renewed way to kindle and let flame our passion for the lives of these holy men and women who have gone before us along the path to heaven. In the cases of the amazing souls profiled in this book, their youthful valor and heroic virtue point to the potential that lies within each of us. Enfolded within these pages are spiritual friends who not only inspire us to lives of greater courage and sanctity by their examples but who also serve as powerful intercessors for those moments when our cares, worries, and concerns simply must be carried directly and immediately to our God, whose love knows no bounds.

What wonderful gifts to be able to share with our loved ones—a road map for spiritual fulfillment, and the promise of holy companionship for those bumps in the road that we'll surely encounter along our way!

Turn the pages of *Radiate* and you'll meet the son of a great chief who turned his back on fame and fortune to pursue his dream of a vocation. You'll come to know a teen whose commitment to her own purity of body and soul cost her the ultimate price. You'll encounter a girl whose greatest desire in life finally came to fruition only after the hour of her death. Along the way, Colleen invites us to bring many of the timeless truths of our faith to life by exploring them with new eyes and open hearts.

Although he lived and died over three quarters of a century before us, Saint Maximilian Kolbe foretold one of the greatest risks to the certainty of our salvation when he said that indifference is deadly. It is the poison that most infiltrates and infects our spirits. The solution to this poison, according to Kolbe, is to praise God, for praise is limitless and will heal our indifference, warming our hearts and in turn helping us to beam brightly for others.

Let's take our marching orders from this martyr who chose death in Christ on his own terms and from the everyday heroes and heroines who are at the heart of this book. In coming to know these amazing souls and what made them so magnificent, let's commit to being the opposite of indifferent in the midst of a society overwhelmed by need and busyness. Let's strive. Let's praise. Let's *Radiate*!

Lisa Hendey,
author of *The Handbook for Catholic Moms*
and *A Book of Saints for Catholic Moms*
(CatholicMom.com
LisaHendey.com)

# Introduction

"Dare to be glowing saints,
in whose eyes and hearts the love of Christ beams
and who thus bring light to the world."

*—Pope Benedict XVI*
*September 25, 2011, Freiburg, Germany*

If you've ever made a truly epic s'more, then you know that the best way to get a marshmallow all gooey on the inside while nice and toasted brown on the outer layer is to have it hang out right around a bed of burning coals for a little while. While the flames of a bonfire grab our attention and pull us in, it is the heat of the embers that continues to consistently radiate warmth, even after the inferno goes down.

The world today offers us so many opportunities and varied ways to burn brightly, letting ourselves shine with the love of Christ. And the stories of the Church's teenage saints show us that, not only are we to burst into flame in his name, but we must work each and every day to keep the fire going, never letting it go out as a result of distraction, confusion, hatred, or laxity. Being a saint is something we must "dare" to do not because the task at hand is easy, but because it is worth it.

Radiating Christ's love and bringing his message to the world is a decision, not simply a feeling or a passing trend. Thus, teenagers profiled in this book span the ages, from the beginning centuries of the Church to within the last one hundred years. Imbued with unique dispositions, talents, and challenges, these young men and women made a choice, oftentimes against great odds, to not just live within the bonds and joys of this world, but to also consider the wonderful promise of eternal life after death.

While encountering the holy people profiled in this book, I invite you to consider not only how powerfully they led lives of virtue but in what ways you are also called to be a radiant conductor of God's promise of eternal life. Just as Paul reminded Timothy "to stir into flame the gift of God that you have…." (2 Timothy 1:6), I likewise encourage you to take the fire of God that you already have in your life, whether it is currently a spark or a bonfire, and make the decision to tend and develop it daily, and share it with all those you encounter.

# HOW TO USE THIS BOOK

**You'll notice when you start to turn these pages** that *Radiate* isn't your ordinary stories-of-the-saints book. I've filled these pages with tons of extras that will bring these zealous young Christians to life and will inspire you to live out your faith with their same fire. The main focus of each chapter is the story of the particular saint. But as you'll see, there is so much more.

**Since our Catholic faith has been practiced** in so many different ways and because the teens featured here come from a variety of times and places, you'll find info and important definitions in the boxes scattered throughout the text. Read up—you just might learn something!

**To help you apply what you're reading to your own life,** I've included reflection questions throughout each story to think and write about. Writing space can be found throughout the book.

**You will also find Scripture verses, pictures, quotes,** and other fun tidbits scattered throughout the stories. Take them in, write them down, think about them for a while—they are all meant to bring the saints to life and inspire you with their holiness!

**At the end of each story is a prayer**, usually one that the person you've just read about said or wrote. Take a moment while you're in a thoughtful mode and inspired by these saintly stories to pray. We know that these men and women are powerful intercessors with God.

**You'll find "Saintly Challenges"** at the end of each chapter. These are ideas of things you can do to connect even deeper with the life of the person you've just read about. There is something for everyone, so dig in.

**At the end of the book** are sources that can help you delve into the teachings that connect to the stories in this book. Remember to check them out!

# SAINT AGNES

# FAITH AND FRIENDSHIP
# WITH CHRIST

"Saint Agnes is one of the famous Roman maidens who demonstrated the genuine beauty of faith in Christ and of friendship with him."

POPE BENEDICT XVI, JANUARY 20, 2012,
ADDRESS TO TEACHERS AND STUDENTS OF THE
ALMO COLLEGIO CAPRANICA

**FEAST DAY:** JANUARY 21

**PATRONAGES:** GARDENERS, BETROTHED COUPLES, CHASTITY, CHILDREN OF MARY, GIRLS, RAPE VICTIMS

**W**hile Saint Agnes has been a heroine of the Church from early in its history, very little of what we know about her is definite. We are certain that she was a young girl living during the reign of the anti-Christian Roman emperors, and that she was one of the earliest Christian martyrs. She is remembered for having offered her virginity to God when she was only about twelve or thirteen years old.

*"While she was a young girl, Agnes had learned that being disciples of the Lord means expressing love for him, staking one's whole life on him. Her dual status—virgin and martyr—reminds us that a credible witness to faith must be a person who lives for Christ, with Christ, and in Christ, transforming his or her life in accordance with the loftiest requirements of giving freely." —Pope Benedict XVI*

Legend has it that Agnes was traveling from school through the streets of Rome when the son of a powerful pagan judge desired her. The young man's parents requested her hand in marriage for their son, accompanying the request with costly gifts. In response, Agnes sent back the gifts, but they persisted by sending a jeweled crown and promising all sorts of other material things. When Agnes continued to decline, her suitor became downright sick due to her refusals. When his parents were told why he was so ill, they appealed to Agnes on his behalf, who in turn told them she had already pledged herself to Someone else!

> **Agnes** means "lamb" in Latin and "chaste" in Greek.

When the young man's father found out Agnes was a Christian and her Someone was Jesus Christ, he told her she could remain a virgin if she would just sacrifice to the goddess of virginity, Vesta. Agnes rejected the deal, so she was forcibly taken to the Vestal altar, where they tried to make her burn in-

> **Agnes** is believed to have lived either during the reign of Roman Emperor Diocletian, putting her martyrdom at about 304, or that of Emperor Decius, c. 254.

> *"Martyrdom—for Saint Agnes—meant generously and freely accepting to spend her young life totally and without reserve to ensure that the Gospel was proclaimed as the truth and beauty that illuminate existence. In Agnes' martyrdom, which she courageously embraced in the Stadium of Domitian, the beauty of belonging to Christ without hesitation and of entrusting ourselves to him shines out forever."—Pope Benedict XVI*

cense for the goddess. When Agnes was made to put out her arms, she instead managed to make the sign of the cross. They ordered her to be sent to a brothel. When Agnes resisted, they took away her clothes so that her only covering was her hair.

Understandably concerned about keeping her naked body covered, she was then forced to walk to the brothel preceded by the ultimate form of humiliation—a town crier—a man whose job it was to yell out to all who would listen her name and exactly where she was going—an ancient form of instant town gossip.

When Agnes arrived at the brothel, an angel was already waiting for her there, so that when her supposed suitor came with his friends to take advantage of her, he became blinded and fell unconscious as soon as he gazed upon her lustfully. This made the judge truly angry, but Agnes asked the Lord for the young man's healing and he cooled down a bit, but not for long. The pagan priests accused the girl of sorcery and, accordingly, a death sentence was handed down from the judge. While sources differ on exactly how she died, with some accounts pointing to death by a sword's decapitation or a burning fire and others saying strangulation, it is agreed upon that, however it was executed, Agnes' was a courageous martyrdom.

**Saint Agnes** was one of the most popular of the early Christian martyrs. As a result, many parents chose the name "Agnes" for their daughters. Reflect on your own birth name. Did your parents name you in honor of someone? What saint did you choose for your confirmation name and why?

**The circumstances** at Saint Agnes' grave became so heated and dangerous that when Agnes' foster sister Emerentiana refused to leave, pagans pelted her with rocks until she was dead. Martyred even before receiving the sacrament of baptism, Emerentiana therefore underwent a baptism of blood. She is a canonized saint as well, and both her entombed remains and feast day remain close to Agnes' own. Saint Emerentiana is commemorated on January 23. A church, the Basilica of Saint Agnes Outside the Walls, was built during Emperor Constantine's reign over the catacomb where she is entombed.

After being buried by her parents in a family grave outside of Rome, the tomb immediately became a Christian shrine, with local pagan officials literally having to chase Christians away from the location.

### Reflection on the pallium Mass by Annie Mitchell

*June 29 is a great holiday in Rome. The streets, which normally bustle with cars and motorbikes, are practically empty on this day, and the huge restless city actually becomes calm and peaceful. It is the feast of Saints Peter and Paul, the great patron saints of Rome.*

*Both Peter and Paul were well beyond their teenage years when Jesus was alive, and grown men when they actually achieved the heroic virtue that led to their sainthood, so what's the connection? It is that on their great feast day the pope distributes the pallium to all metropolitan archbishops who were appointed to office during the past year.*

*The pallium is a scarf-like vestment that is placed on the shoulders of an archbishop as a symbol of his office. There is a rich symbolism in the process to create the pallium, and it begins on the Feast of Saint Agnes of Rome. Pallia are made from lambs' wool, and the lambs that will provide this wool are specially blessed by the pope on the Feast of Saint Agnes—who has traditionally been associated with lambs because her name sounds very much like the Latin word "agnus." After being blessed by the pope, the lambs are*

*sent to an Italian convent where the sisters use the wool to weave each
vestment. As a crowning step in the process, each finished pallium
is placed on top of the relics of Saint Peter and waits there for the
pallium Mass on June 29. Hence, on the great Roman holiday—the
feast of Saints Peter and Paul—the symbolism is complete. When the
pope places the pallium on the shoulders of each new archbishop,
the lamb's wool represents the sheep that he takes upon his shoulders as he assumes the care of his archdiocese—just like the Good
Shepherd. Because his pallium rested on top the relics of our first
pope, it also reminds us of the archbishop's unbroken connection
to the pope—the successor of Saint Peter who bestows it upon him.*

*Many of the new archbishops who travel to Rome for the pal-
lium Mass also lead a pilgrimage for the people in his new flock.
This was how I ended up in Saint Peter's Basilica on June 29, 2010.
I was a member of the group led to Rome by Archbishop Dennis
Schnurr, the new head of the Archdiocese of Cincinnati. He was one
of thirty-eight men to receive his pallium from Pope Benedict XVI,
and he took us, his spiritual flock, along with him on the journey.
Just being in Rome gave me a real sense of our universal Church,
and I was particularly aware of this during the pallium celebrations:
some of the new archbishops who would receive their pallium had
only to travel a few hours from different parts of Italy, but many
more had come from places as far away as Korea, the Philippines,
Colombia and Angola; not to mention Cincinnati, Miami, and
Milwaukee.*

*The celebration of the feast day actually began the night before
with vespers at the Basilica of Saint Paul Outside the Walls. Though
I didn't realize it at the time (the Holy Father usually reads his homi-
lies in Italian, and my Italian wasn't that good), Pope Benedict used
this occasion to make a major announcement: he was establishing
the Pontifical Council for the New Evangelization which would be
dedicated to revitalizing our faith in areas where Catholics have
grown complacent. He spoke of it beautifully that evening:*

> "The Church is an immense force for renewal in the world. This is not, of course, because of her own strength but because of the power of the Gospel in which the Holy Spirit of God breathes, God Creator and Redeemer of the world. The challenges of the present time—the historical and social and, especially, the spiritual challenges—are certainly beyond the human capacity."

Certainly the archbishops who received their palliums the next afternoon (and all bishops, who are the successors to the apostles) are an integral part of the pope's plan, and necessary to bring about this New Evangelization. But we are just as critical, and each of us is called to participate. Our bishops and priests can only get so far and will never have the same opportunities that we do to reach the people who are part of our everyday lives. If we pray to be given the zeal of Saints Peter, Paul, and Agnes, there is always a chance that we can spark something wonderful in our friends and family who have fallen away. When the Holy Spirit works in our lives, we can set the world ablaze.

**The pallium** "...is woven from the wool of lambs blessed on the feast of Saint Agnes. Thus it reminds us of the Shepherd who himself became a lamb, out of love for us. It reminds us of Christ, who set out through the mountains and the deserts, in which his lamb, humanity, had strayed. It reminds us of him who took the lamb—humanity—me— upon his shoulders, in order to carry me home.

*—Pope Benedict XVI, June 29, 2011, homily during holy Mass for the Imposition of the Sacred Pallium on Metropolitan Archbishops*

## Catechetical Connection: Jesus the Paschal Lamb

Saint Agnes is often depicted in art with a lamb, to symbolize her innocence and virgin martyrdom.

"The Lamb who takes away the sin of the world" (*Catechism of the Catholic Church* 608).

After agreeing to baptize him along with the sinners, John the Baptist looked at Jesus and pointed him out as the "Lamb of God, who takes away the sin of the world." By doing so, he reveals that Jesus is at the same time the suffering Servant who silently allows himself to be led to the slaughter and who bears the sin of the multitudes, and also the Paschal Lamb, the symbol of Israel's redemption at the first Passover. Christ's whole life expresses his mission: "to serve, and to give his life as a ransom for many."

**Paschal:** A term referring to Easter or Passover

*Have you ever known someone who took on a burden, such as a punishment or gossip, even though he or she was innocent of any wrongdoing? Recount the situation.*

*"Agnes also sealed in martyrdom the other crucial element of her life, virginity for Christ and for the Church. Indeed, the conscious, free, and mature choice of virginity testifies to the wish to belong totally to Christ and paves the way to the total gift of self in martyrdom. If martyrdom is a heroic final act, virginity is the result of a long friendship with Jesus, developed in constant listening to his word, in the dialogue of prayer, in the eucharistic encounter."*
—Pope Benedict XVI

## PRAYER TO SAINT AGNES

*Saint Agnes,*
*You lived in a land hostile to the message of the Lord.*
*Aid me in following your example*
*in always standing up for the gospel,*
*even when it gets difficult.*
*Give me the strength to be a witness*
*to both sexual purity and the sacrificial love of Jesus Christ.*
*Amen.*

## MEMORY VERSE
### JOHN 1:29

The next day he saw Jesus coming toward him
and said, "Behold, the Lamb of God,
who takes away the sin of the world."

*Look up John 1 in your Bible. Name the person who says, "Behold, the Lamb of God, who takes away the sin of the world." After verse 29, what else does the speaker say about Jesus?*

_____

_____

_____

_____

# Saintly Challenges

- Take some time to meditate on this English translation of an age-old hymn. According to tradition, Saint Ambrose penned the hymn *Agnes beatae virginis* ("blessed virgin Agnes") in honor of the saint's boldness in pursuit of virtue.

## AGNES BEATAE VIRGINIS

The blessed virgin Agnes flies
back to her home above the skies,
and she is born in heav'n above
because she gave her blood in love.

Mature enough to give her life,
though still too young to be a wife,
what joy she shows when death appears
that one would think: her bridegroom nears!

> **Saint Ambrose (374–397):** A doctor of the Church, Ambrose was a fourth-century Christian bishop whose eloquent preaching converted many, including Saint Augustine. In his book *Confessions*, Saint Augustine recalls being astonished at walking into Saint Ambrose's quarters and finding him reading silently. At that time in history, almost all people read books aloud, even when they were by themselves!

Her captors lead her to the fire
but she refuses their desire,
"For it is not such smold'ring brands
Christ's virgins take into their hands."

"This flaming fire of pagan rite
extinguishes all faith and light.
Then stab me here, so that the flood
may overcome this hearth in blood."

And she was stabbed,
and she was brave,
and dying, further witness gave,
for as she fell on bended knee
she wrapped her robes in modesty.

O Virgin-born, all praises be
to You throughout eternity.
and unto everlasting days
to Father and the Spirit, praise.

**Saint Ambrose**

---

**Sward:** A grassy area of land

---

- Check out Lord Alfred Tennyson's poem *Saint Agnes' Eve*,
  where the poem's narrator, a religious sister, contemplates
  meeting Christ in his heavenly glory.

## SAINT AGNES' EVE

Deep on the convent-roof the snows
    Are sparkling to the moon:
My breath to heaven like vapour goes:
    May my soul follow soon!

The shadows of the convent-towers
    Slant down the snowy sward,
Still creeping with the creeping hours
    That lead me to my Lord:
Make Thou my spirit pure and clear
    As are the frosty skies,
Or this first snowdrop of the year
    That in my bosom lies.

As these white robes are soil'd and dark,
    To yonder shining ground;
As this pale taper's earthly spark,
    To yonder argent round;
So shows my soul before the Lamb,
    My spirit before Thee;
So in mine earthly house I am,
    To that I hope to be.
Break up the heavens, O Lord! and far,
    Thro' all yon starlight keen,
Draw me, thy bride, a glittering star,
    In raiment white and clean.

He lifts me to the golden doors;
    The flashes come and go;
All heaven bursts her starry floors,
    And strows her lights below,
And deepens on and up! the gates
    Roll back, and far within
For me the Heavenly Bridegroom waits,
    To make me pure of sin.
The sabbaths of Eternity,
    One sabbath deep and wide -
A light upon the shining sea -
    The Bridegroom with his bride!

# SAINTS GABRIEL OF DUISCO, LOUIS IBARAKI, JUAN SOAN OF GOTO, AND THOMAS KOZAKI

## JAPANESE MARTYRS

## COURAGE AND STEADFASTNESS

"…The early centuries of Christianity in Japan were indelibly marked by the courage and steadfastness of your martyrs."

—POPE JOHN PAUL II, MARCH 31, 2001,
ADDRESS OF JOHN PAUL II TO THE BISHOPS OF JAPAN

**FEAST DAY:** FEBRUARY 3

**B**y the year 1587, there were about 200,000 Christians in Japan. However it was in that same year that an order was passed by a Buddhist priest named Nichijoshonin to oppress these followers of Jesus, resulting in the destruction of 140 churches, twenty-six religious orders' houses, and the expulsion of Christian missionaries from the country. Nonetheless, over the next ten years, 100,000 more people courageously converted to Christianity in spite of the social and physical dangers that could await them. And await them they did.

In 1593, missionaries from modern-day Spain traveled via the Philippines to join in ministering with 130 Jesuits already working for the faith in Japan. These newcomers were less cautious about abiding by the edict against Christianity than those more familiar with the complicated situation. Regrettably, their relative lack of discretion came not long before a Spanish ship was wrecked onto the Japanese coast with artillery on board. In the heat of the moment, with the Japanese authorities already on alert due to the weaponry on the ship, the Spanish boat captain falsely boasted that Spain, and specifically Spaniards already there, was preparing to take over Japan. This furthered the peril that the Spanish missionaries to Japan had put themselves in.

**When Saint Francis Xavier** went to Japan as a missionary, he found his greatest success in Nagasaki, which became the epicenter of Japanese Catholicism. You may also recall that one of the two atomic bombs dropped on Japan by the United States at the end of World War II landed in Nagasaki, killing many Christians and non-Christians alike. There was a community of Jesuit priests who lived less than a mile from the detonation point, and miraculously, while every other building in their vicinity was flattened, their rectory, as well as all eight priests, survived relatively unscathed. Similarly, a Franciscan friary close to where the bomb was dropped was spared because a mountain stood between it and the explosion. Father Hubert Schiffer, one of the Jesuit priests who survived the bombing, believed his community's daily recitation of the rosary was the reason they weren't vaporized by the nuclear explosion that destroyed everything else in its path.

15

In 1597, all-out tyranny raged against Christians. Lists had been made of known Christians, but the intimidation was turned up several notches when six Franciscan missionaries and twenty Japanese Christians were taken by order of Toyotomi Hideyoshi to make a very serious point. These Christians embarked on a thirty-day forced march from Kyoto to Urakami, located in the northern part of the island of Nagasaki, to Mount Mubonzan (now known as Mount Kompira), which overlooks Nagasaki City.

The twenty-six chosen by Toyotomi Hideyoshi to suffer because they were living as Christians included three teenagers and a twelve-year-old: Saint Louis Ibaraki was twelve, Saint Thomas Kozaki was fourteen, and Saints Gabriel and Juan Soan were both nineteen. Louis had been born in the Owari province of Japan

**Apostasize/Apostasy:** To give up one's Christian beliefs

and was the nephew of Paul Ibaraki and Leo Karasumaru, both of whom were also forced to march. The cheerful boy could not be convinced to apostasize and held the important task of keeping the others' spirits up through singing songs and being joyful, to the extent that Father Francis Blanco remarked, "We have little Louis with us and he is so full of courage and in such high spirits that it astonishes everybody."

*Name a situation in your life where you can model joy in the midst of difficulty, as Saint Louis Ibaraki did.*

Not much older than Louis was Saint Thomas Kozaki, who was from Ise and helped his carpenter father with projects at the Franciscan monastery. Thomas Kozaki is perhaps best known for the poignant letter he wrote to his mother saying goodbye. Saint Gabriel also hailed from Ise and had previously worked as a page in the city of Kyoto. Gabriel was a Christian catechist. Saint Juan Soan was from the Goto Islands, which are off the coast of Nagasaki. He grew up in a Christian family and was educated by Jesuits in Nagasaki, where he was training as a catechist-artist there. Juan worked under the guidance of a priest in the Japanese city of Osaka.

Before these Christians left Kyoto, their left ears were cut off. And by the time they reached Urakami, their hands were bound and the twenty-six men and boys were separated into three groups, each one led by a Franciscan reciting the rosary. When his rosary was requested from Brother Francis of Saint Michael as a relic, he responded, "Sorry, wait a little more. I have not finished yet." When they reached Nagasaki City, they were led to Nishizaka (Martyrs') Hill, the lowest hill off the side of Mount Mubonzan. Instead of being led to where criminals were typically executed, however, a Portuguese Christian had asked that they be taken to a nearby wheat field, instead. Terazawa Hazaburo, the man appointed executioner, agreed. Terazawa was the brother of the governor and a friend of the Japanese Jesuit Paul Miki, one of the men led on the march from Kyoto. While he did not believe the martyrs de-

**Catechist:** A Christian religion teacher

**Saint Paul Miki**

served their punishment, he was too afraid of Taikosama to openly object. Still, he allowed Jesuit Fathers Pasio and Rodriguez to accompany the men. On the morning of February 5, 1597, Juan Soan took Jesuit vows, knowing his life and those of the other twenty-five Christians would be coming to an end that day. After reaching Nishizaka Hill, a death sentence was posted on the handle of a lance that was speared into the ground:

"As these men came from the Philippines under the guise of ambassadors, and chose to stay in Miyako preaching the Christian law, which I have severely forbidden all these years, I come to decree that they be put to death, together with the Japanese that have accepted that law."

17

In response, Paul Miki, another of the twenty-six martyrs who was a Jesuit, courageously proclaimed, "I did not come from the Philippines, I am a Japanese by birth, and a brother of the Society of Jesus. I have committed no crime, and the only reason why I am put to death is that I have been teaching the doctrine of our Lord Jesus Christ. I am very happy to die for such a cause and see my death as a great blessing from the Lord. At this critical time, when you can rest assured that I will not try to deceive you, I want to stress and make it unmistakably clear that man can find no way to salvation other than the Christian way."

The method by which the men were to be put to death was a fitting testimony to their valiant faith in Christ. One by one, crosses had been prepared to fit each individual martyr, with the majority of the crosses standing over six and a half feet tall. When the Christians reached the wheat field where the crosses were already prepared for them, Brother Philip Gonzalo literally clasped his with tenderness, serving as a model for the others to do the same. Iron fastenings would be used on most of the martyrs to hold down their necks, arms and legs, with a rope then tied around the waist. That being said, Father Peter Bautista, a Spanish Franciscan in their number, asked his captor, in reference to his hands and feet, to "nail them down, brother," to better mirror the death of his Savior.

**Saint Paul Miki (1562–1597):** A Jesuit seminarian, Paul was brought up in a prosperous Japanese family. He is considered to be one of the major leaders of the twenty-six martyrs.

*Which of Jesus' sufferings would you be willing to undergo for the sake of the gospel? Which would you fear the most? What appreciation does this give you for the courage of the martyrs of Nagasaki?*

**The Martyrs of Nagasaki** were not the only ones who were crucified like Jesus; the Apostle Peter and his brother Andrew suffered similar fates, with a twist. Tradition holds that Saint Peter requested that he be crucified upside down because he didn't consider himself worthy of the same fate as Jesus, while Saint Andrew was crucified on an X-shaped cross. The Saint Andrew cross is the official symbol of Scotland, represented on their flag in white against a blue background.

When it came time for the martyrs to enter eternal life on Nishizaka Hill, Louis repeatedly intoned, "Paradise, paradise...Jesus, Mary!" from his smallest of crosses, before they were all simultaneously speared with a long blade on the end of a lance, which was thrust into their chests. The executioner Terazawa was in tears after the executions.

The following year, in 1598, a group of Christians from the Philippines was allowed by Toyotomi Hideyoshi to take the relics of the martyrs' deceased bodies and their crosses. Christians then filled the holes left by the crosses with flowering trees, building a large cross in the middle of them. Each Friday night, they would sing songs and adorn the trees with candles, remembering the martyrs' sacrifices for the faith.

*"I can tell Your Reverence that these deaths have been a special gift of Divine Providence to this church. Up to now our persecutor had not gone to the extreme of shedding Christian blood. Our teaching therefore had been mostly theoretical without the corroborating evidence of dying for our Christian faith. But now, seeing by experience these remarkable and most extraordinary deaths, it is beyond belief how much our new Christians have been strengthened, how much encouragement they have received to do the same themselves." —Excerpt from a letter from Father Francis Calderon, Jesuit missionary*

# A CHURCH UNDERGROUND

By 1619, the ruler was Tokugawa Ieyasu, and the trees that had been planted in the places where the crosses had been were cut down. The backlash against Christians had again escalated, and at least 650 individuals were martyred on Nishizaka Hill and the vicinity. The church then went underground until March 17, 1865, when Commodore Matthew C. Perry entered Japan and found that, after almost 250 years, there was still evidence of Christianity, with estimates of 20,000 people still secretly practicing the faith. In 1873, Japanese Christians were finally allowed the freedom of religion. It is estimated that there are a total of 1,200 Japanese Christian martyrs altogether.

> **Tradition** holds that the centurion who stood watch at Jesus' crucifixion went on to become a saint. Saint Longinus is considered the man whose spear pierced the side of Christ, and that relic has been the source of many legends.

## Catechetical Connection:
## Christ Offered Himself on the Cross for all Humanity

The twenty-six Japanese martyrs not only gave up their lives for eternal life in Christ, but they did it in a fashion very similar to the Savior himself: on wooden crosses. So what makes their sacrifices different from the ultimate sacrifice of Christ? What's the difference between being a martyr and being the Savior of the world? This excerpt from the *Catechism of the Catholic Church* tells us that his death on the cross was unique, giving us a gift that is truly lifesaving and available to all people.

"Jesus consummates his sacrifice on the cross" (*CCC* 616).

"It is love 'to the end' that confers on Christ's sacrifice its value as redemption and reparation as atonement and satisfaction. He knew and loved us all when he offered his life. Now 'the love of Christ controls us, because we are convinced that one has died for all; therefore all have died.' No man, not even the holiest, was ever able to take on himself the sins of all men and offer himself as a sacrifice for all. The existence in Christ of the divine person of the Son, who at once surpasses and embraces all human persons, and constitutes himself as the head of all mankind, makes possible his redemptive sacrifice for all" (*CCC* 616).

*Think back on a time when someone made a sacrifice for you. How does/did the person's sacrifice bring meaning to yours?*

**Reparation:** Making up for wrongdoing

_____

_____

*How is the cross depicted in art at your parish? Recall and write the details here.*

_____

_____

*Name a Catholic saint other than the Japanese martyrs who was crucified.*

_____

_____

## PRAYER TO THE TEENAGE JAPANESE MARTYRS SAINTS GABRIEL, LOUIS, JUAN SOAN, AND THOMAS,

*You not only gave your lives for love of Christ,
but emulated him by dying brutally on a cross.
Help me to die to my sins each and every day, and, when crosses
come my way, to embrace them as a means of growing
in closer union with our Savior.
Inspire me to never take for granted the ability to freely practice my
faith, and give me the courage to always proclaim
the name of Jesus, especially in the midst of hardship.
Thank you for the gift of your witness.
Amen.*

SAINTS GABRIEL OF ᶜDUISCO, LOUIS IBARAKI, JUAN SOAN OF GOTO, AND THOMAS KOZAKI

# MEMORY VERSE
## PHILIPPIANS 2:8

"...He humbled himself, becoming obedient to death,
even death on a cross."

*If Christ could be obedient to the Father and die on the cross, then we can surely take up our little, daily crosses. How have you taken up Christ's cross and followed in his steps today?*

_____

_____

_____

_____

_____

_____

## Saintly Challenges

- Because they underwent martyrdom as a group, the Martyrs of Nagasaki were able to encourage one another in the face of death. Evaluate how your friendships with fellow Christians are serving to give you strength in the midst of a culture hostile to faith.

# SAINT BERNADETTE

## A SIMPLE YOUNG GIRL

"...A simple young girl from Lourdes, Bernadette Soubirous, saw a light, and in this light she saw a young lady who was 'beautiful, more beautiful than any other.'"

—POPE BENEDICT XVI, SEPTEMBER 13, 2008, TORCHLIGHT PROCESSION HOMILY, LOURDES, FRANCE

**FEAST DAY:** APRIL 16

**PATRONAGE**: BODILY ILLNESS; SHEPHERDS AND SHEPHERDESSES; AGAINST POVERTY; PEOPLE RIDICULED FOR FAITH; LOURDES, FRANCE

In 1858, Mary appeared a total of eighteen times in a grotto used as a shelter by pigs. Perhaps even more amazingly, the person she came to see was a four-foot-seven-inch-tall girl named Bernadette, who was unable to read, write, or speak French. Instead, she spoke a regional dialect of her native Lourdes and had been accused of being "incapable of learning" such an extent that her catechist wanted to delay her reception of her first holy Communion.

At age eleven, Bernadette contracted cholera, which affected her growth. She had to deal with profound asthma and, later, tuberculosis in her lungs and bones. This explains why her sister Marie and friend Jeanne cried out when crossing the very cold water where the River Gave and the mill water converged. If they thought the water was much too frigid, they figured sickly Bernadette didn't have a chance of making it across to follow them. It was cold as ice, and being subjected to wading through water like that was one of the last things Bernadette needed to be doing, as her mother regularly reminded her.

Bernadette was initially afraid of the "Lady" surrounded by white light, with her blue eyes, white dress, blue belt, white veil, one gold rose on each foot, and holding a rosary with white beads. In fact, she wondered if the Lady could possibly be real. She finally got her rosary out of her pocket and tried to make the sign of the cross but couldn't.

**How does the Church** discern whether visions of Mary are valid or fake? For instance, how do we know the difference between Bernadette's vision and a fictitious story? Since 1974, the Vatican's Congregation for the Doctrine of the Faith has used very specific criteria to evaluate reported Marian apparitions. The questions the Church considers include such data as: What is the mental state of the person reporting the apparition? Does the message conflict with Church teaching? Does this appear to be an attempt on the part of the supposed visionary to gain money off of the gullibility of others?

Bernadette was so fearful that she couldn't move. The Lady then made the sign of the cross with her own rosary, and Bernadette was able to mirror her and felt calmed. The girl then kneeled down and continued to pray the rosary, and the Lady moved her fingers along the beads but did not move her own lips. When they finished, the Lady gestured for Bernadette to come closer, but she stayed back and the Lady left.

Bernadette reunited with her sister and friend, and she questioned them about what they had seen. Her sister and friend were confused and stated they hadn't seen anything at all. Trying to keep her cool, Bernadette initially denied that anything had been out of the ordinary. Eventually, though, Bernadette relented and told her friends about her encounter, asking them to promise that nothing would be mentioned to anyone else. Marie and Jeanne, however, thought that the Lady meant to do them ill and suggested that Bernadette not go back to see her. Bernadette insisted that the Lady did not have any bad intentions. Whatever their reasons, the girls broke their promise to Bernadette when they arrived home. This resulted in being forbidden by Louise (Bernadette and Marie's mother) to make any more trips to the grotto.

*Reflect on a time when you had your confidence betrayed. Were you hurt by the incident? Did the person(s) at least have good intentions?*

---------------------------------------------------------------

---------------------------------------------------------------

---------------------------------------------------------------

The next Sunday, Bernadette promised her mother she wouldn't fall into the water and would be home for vespers if she could just go down to the grotto for a bit. Her mother concedes as Bernadette promised to be very careful and be back to the family home in time for prayer. After being given permission, she proceeded with other village girls to the grotto, still partially second-guessing what she had previously experienced.

It is crucial to Bernadette's story to remember that she obeys her parents always, even when they misunderstand the Lady's intentions. Was there ever a time when you had to be obedient to your parents, knowing that they had your best interest at heart, even though it was difficult?

After praying one decade of the rosary, she saw the Lady and, prepared, began to throw holy water on her! Bernadette's rationale was that if she wasn't of God, she would go away. Far from simply disappearing, the Lady smiled, lowered her head and beckoned to Bernadette, who started to become fearful. The apparition discontinued when Bernadette finished praying the rosary.

The following Thursday, Bernadette came to the grotto with a different kind of reinforcement: adults. They told Bernadette to take a pen and paper and ask: "If you have something to say to me, would you be kind enough to write it down?" The Lady answered that this was not necessary and responded with an invitation back to the grotto for fifteen more visits. This request was made with such kindness and politeness that Bernadette, an impoverished teenager with little to no education, was taken aback.

*Think of the people in your own life who aren't used to being treated in accordance with their God-given worth as human beings. What can you do to better pay them the respect they deserve?*

On a subsequent visit, Bernadette was asked to drink and wash in the grotto's spring water. The young girl thought the Lady was referring to the Gave River, as she did not know of a spring, and was surprised to see her indicate a space under the grotto. The space that our Lady referred was a little muddied water, barely enough to be scooped up. When Bernadette attempted to drink it, she vomited the first three times and finally drank a bit down.

*Appearances can be deceiving. When was the last time you were surprised to find beauty or goodness in an unexpected place?*

As Bernadette continued to visit the Lady at the grotto, she followed the Lady's requests to kiss and crawl on the ground for the salvation of sinners, as well as to pray for their conversion with a marked humility; not for the increasing amount of attention that was being drawn to the simple place. It was becoming clear to all involved that the message of Lourdes would be one of penance and, soon enough, healing.

The practice of lighting a candle at the Lourdes Grotto began when Bernadette started to bring a blessed, lighted candle. This practice continues today as surely as the miracles that flow from the place, such as in the case of Catherine Latapie, a woman from Lourdes whose paralyzed arm healed after bathing in the grotto's spring on Monday, March 1, 1858, within the period of time that our Lady was still visiting Bernadette.

Shortly thereafter, the Lady had a message for Bernadette to deliver to the local priests: Build a chapel and hold processions at the grotto. Bernadette saw Father Peyramale to go about fulfilling the request. This priest asked her to find out who exactly this Lady was and report back to him with the information. When Bernadette did inquire of the

"I am the Immaculate Conception."

Lady's name, she simply answered with a smile, which made Bernadette's priest think that the Lady was making a mockery of the girl and that she shouldn't go back to the grotto. After the fifteen promised visits, having been asked four times, the Lady told Bernadette who she was and continues to be: "I am the Immaculate Conception." This title was so unfamiliar to Bernadette that she was afraid she would forget it, so she repeated it over and over again to herself on the way back home. While Father Peyramale didn't initially believe that Mary announced, "I am the

Immaculate Conception," thinking a person couldn't be an event, he eventually became one of Bernadette's biggest supporters and greatest friends.

The last Marian apparition to Bernadette at Lourdes was on July 16, 1858. Bernadette was forced to pray in a field across from the river because the grotto had been blocked off by the police. To Bernadette, though, it made no difference, as, "It seemed to me that I was at the grotto, at the same distance as the other times. All I could see was the Virgin. I had never seen her so beautiful."

Over the eighteen visits with the Lady, Bernadette was given three messages that were to be for her ears only, while also being told that "she did not promise to make me happy in this world, but in the next." While we still do not know what the messages entailed, it was certainly true that Bernadette's earthly journey wouldn't be easy.

The Sunday following Bernadette's final visits with the Lady, the young girl was taken by the police during her departure from the church and interrogated. After being threatened by a tour of the local prison, she was brought into the chambers of the police commissioner and asked to recite the occurrence of events at the grotto. When Bernadette realized the recounted story had been recorded incorrectly, she pointed out the discrepancies. She argued her point over the validity of her own statements the problematic errors being recorded in the account for an hour and a half. Meanwhile, her father and other villagers clamored outside for her release, banging entryways and windows, shouting, "If you don't let her leave, we will kick the door in." Bernadette was finally released by the police commissioner, but her trouble with the local authorities wasn't over yet.

Later that same week, she was interrogated by the office of the imperial prosecutor and was made to recount the same sequence of events yet again, but this time her mother was present. Crowds were again at the entryways and windows, refusing to desist until the pair were allowed to leave. Both mother and daughter were forced to stand while being interrogated, and yet again errors were recorded in the official account. Bernadette was accused of having her current story conflict with the earlier version from the police commissioner, but she denied this while the police commissioner threatened imprisonment. As a result, her mother broke down and cried. At this, the imperial prosecutor, realizing perhaps that he had gone too far, finally offered them chairs on which to sit. While her mother Louise accepted, Bernadette courageously said her thanks and sat cross-legged on the floor rather than accept a chair from the men who were doubting the authenticity of her story. It is notable that Bernadette never changed her story in official recordings of her experience.

Bernadette wrote many letters for a girl with a limited amount of education until the middle of her teen years. In the fall of 1858, she entered into a school with the Sisters of Charity and Christian Instruction in Lourdes. It was there that she started to learn to read, write, and speak French. Despite her education, throughout her life, sisters would proofread her correspondence before she rewrote letters and sent them out. By 1860, Bernadette was continuing her schooling and lived with the sisters. There was an the influx of pilgrims visiting Lourdes while Bernadette concentrated on her studies. The interest of pilgrims

The rock cave at Massabielle, where Saint Bernadette Soubirous claimed to have seen the Blessed Virgin Mary. Now it is a religious grotto.

would conflict with her daily tasks of working in the infirmary and with the younger students. For the rest of her life, this would pose a challenge, with Bernadette commenting that, "All I do is receive pilgrims from morning to night," and that she was "weary of seeing so many people." From the beginning of the apparitions, Bernadette—later Sister Marie-Bernarde—was humble. She refused to accept presents, whether in the form of money or otherwise, from pilgrims to Lourdes, and she deflected glory and prestige from herself to the primary message of Our Lady as given at the grotto in Lourdes, France: a call to penance and renewal.

Not only pilgrims were interested in Bernadette's encounters with Mary, the beautiful Lady, but also the Church. The Bishop of Tarbes, Monsignor Laurence, questioned Bernadette about the apparitions between November 17, 1858, and December 7, 1860, and finally made a joyous announcement on January 18, 1862, that the diocese had officially approved the Lourdes apparitions and messages.

Being a follower of Christ does not guarantee everything going your way without hardships. This was especially true for Bernadette, who suffered from non-stop illness throughout her life. Due to her illness, Bernadette received Last Rites a total of four times, the first time occurring when she was still a teenager on April 28, 1862. It is amazing, though, that she never felt sorry for herself through her earliest trials and later through serious asthma attacks and a bout with pneumonia. Instead, she poured her heart into caring for her family and friends, especially through her letters and prayers, saying, "I will not forget anyone" in her petitions to the Lord through the intercessions of his Mother.

While she felt the call to religious life, she was unsure of what particular order she should join. Even though she had been invited by several different ones, she was worried that her health conditions would make her ineligible. Her worries turned out to be well-founded. Mother Louise Ferrand, the superior general of the Sisters of Charity and Christian Instruction, objected for this very reason, saying: "she does not know how to do anything." Fortunately, she was not the one to make the final decision, as on July 7, 1866, Bernadette was accepted into the Congregation of the Sisters of Charity and Christian Instruction and joined as a postulant.

*Recount a time when you had to make a decision on what path to take, whether it be spiritually, educationally, athletically, etc.*

Not everyone had such negative feelings toward Bernadette's entrance into the community life. According to the community's official journal, "At last our prayers have been answered! Bernadette is in the novitiate! How anxious we have been to have this privileged visionary of the Grotto of Lourdes among us! She is exactly as she is reputed to be: humble, simple, modest, smiling and sweetly happy in spite of her long illnesses." The very next day after she arrived, Bernadette personally told the community her experiences with the apparitions conditionally, as she demanded that it would be the only time and she wouldn't be asked about it again. Later that same month, on July 29, 1866, she took the habit and became Sister Marie-Bernarde, in honor of the special Lady and Saint Bernard, her patron saint.

She took on the humble work of assisting as a nurse in the infirmary, but the public still sought after her, and bishops visited her. Many requested pictures, as this was the beginning of an era when photography was made possible. But Bernadette was afforded relative peace in the convent, especially with the protection of her mother superior. When the public asked the order for Bernadette's prayers, these intentions were wisely brought before and prayed by all the women of her community, as she was living a communal religious life.

A description of Sister Marie-Bernarde from her doctor sums up her nature throughout her time with the sisters. The doctor noted that "she is a small, rather sickly looking, twenty-seven-year-old woman. She has a calm and gentle nature, and she cares for her patients with a great deal of intelligence. She carries out every order impeccably; hence, she inspires respect and she has my entire confidence. As you can see, this young sister is far from insane. I shall go further: her calm, simple, and gentle nature does not dispose her in the least to being susceptible to insanity." In October 1866, she again received Last Rites, and due to the severity of her condition made religious vows. Thereafter, she was confined to the infirmary for four months. Later that year, her mother died, and the following October, she made her first profession (restating the vows that were given during Last Rites).

*in articulo mortis* (at the point of death).

The year 1870 brought the Franco-Prussian War, and the sisters cared for wounded Frenchmen. Even with so many immediate cares occupying her time, Bernadette was most concerned for her siblings, especially her youngest brother and godson, Pierre, who she was unable to see for the entirety of time that she was away at the convent. In 1871, her brother was an eleven-and-a-half-year-old junior high school student in a family that had just lost their father. Bernadette wrote to him frequently to inquire about how things were at home and how her brother was coming along with his studies, an opportunity that she had not been able to have at his age. Similarly, she advised her younger cousin Bernadette that "you will surely be happy if you love the dear Lord who protects you in a special way by allowing you to receive a Christian education. There are so many who do not enjoy the same advantage as you."

*Do you take your education in the faith for granted? Who is an individual who has helped guide your path in Christ?*

---

---

---

---

Sometimes, as is the case with practically all human beings, the people who Bernadette cared for the most frustrated and let her down. She would become annoyed when family members, especially her brothers and sisters, did not return her letters, or, even worse, when she was "told that my letters are circulating everywhere. It hurt me so much to discover this and if it happens again I will not write anyone anymore." Additionally, her brother Jean-Marie entered religious life but later did not tell Sister Marie-Bernarde when he left or even when he eventually married. She was deeply wounded, feeling hurt to have to find out the news from others.

*Has someone reached out to you, perhaps via social media, that you have not taken the time to respond to? Take the chance to remake that connection.*

---

---

---

In 1874, Sister Marie-Bernarde became an assistant to the sacristan, however from October 1875 to July 1876, the only chapel she was able to find herself was the one she referred to as her "White Chapel," which was better known as her infirmary bed. So sick that she could not even go to Mass, she nonetheless kept up her spirits, writing, "What can I do but be patient and keep saying: Fiat!" Her sickness continued for the last years of her young life, but her faithfulness to her vocation continued to the end, as she took her perpetual vows on September 22, received Last Rites for the last time on March 28, and finally passed at 3:15 p.m. on April 16, 1879, at the age of thirty-five. Her last words underlie that, at heart, Sister Marie-Bernarde was still the simple young girl a beautiful Lady had appeared to: "Pray for me, a poor sinner!"

> **Sacristan:** A person who prepares the things needed for Mass

> **Fiat:** Let it be done

---

*Ask Jesus, our Savior, to come prepare a place for himself in your young hearts so there will be nothing to grieve him when he arrives. Think only of Jesus, since he is choosing to rest in your souls. Make his dwelling place like a sanctuary of innocence and peace.*

---

## Catechetical Connection: Vocation

From Sister Marie-Bernarde Soubirous to her brother Pierre: "Have you made a decision about your vocation? What do you plan to do? Dear friend, you have no idea how interested I am in the welfare of your soul. Not a day passes that I do not pray for you to our Lord and to the most holy Virgin to give you discernment about your vocation and to show you God's holy will. This is not the kind of decision we make overnight; it is for the rest of our lives and usually our eternal happiness depends on our vocation. So pray much, dear friend, that God will show you the choice you should make, both for love of him and for your own salvation."

Just as it has strict guidelines for approving Marian apparitions, the Church is also very careful when it comes to officially approving miracles. Since Lourdes is known to be a site where many healing miracles have been reported, it has become a place the Church has paid special attention to since Bernadette's visions. Well over 6,000 miracles have been reported from Lourdes pilgrims, but the Church has only approved a few dozen. In order to be approved, a reported case has to be reviewed by panels of theologians, doctors, and Church officials to make sure that what has taken place is authentically miraculous. After all, think of the scandal that would be caused if an approved miracle was later found out to be a fraud!

## The *Catechism of the Catholic Church*: The Vocation of Lay People

"Lay believers are in the front line of Church life; for them the Church is the animating principle of human society. Therefore, they in particular ought to have an ever-clearer consciousness not only of belonging to the Church, but of being the Church, that is to say, the community of the faithful on earth under the leadership of the Pope, the common Head, and of the bishops in communion with him. They are the Church" (*CCC* 899).

*For the most part, the apostolate of pastors cannot be fully effective without the activity of:*

_____

_____

_____

## PRAYER WITH BERNADETTE:

*O my God, I do not ask you to keep me from suffering
but to be with me in affliction.
Teach me to seek you as my only comforter;
sustain my faith; strengthen my hope; purify my love.
Grant me the grace to recognize your hand in the midst of suffering
and to want no other comforter than you.
Amen.*

## MEMORY VERSE

### JEREMIAH 17:13

"O Hope of Israel, LORD!
all who forsake you shall be put to shame;
The rebels shall be enrolled in the netherworld;
they have forsaken the LORD,
source of living waters."

*Do you ever ignore your commitments to God? How so?*

_____

_____

_____

_____

_____

*Bernadette's advice to her seventeen-year-old brother Pierre:*

"I implore you not to spend time with young people
who have a bad influence on you. It will do you harm
without you even suspecting it."

# Saintly Challenges

- Keep a rosary handy in your pocket, purse, car, etc., imitating Bernadette on the first day she saw the apparition of Mary at the Grotto of Lourdes.

- Bernadette used her letter writing as a way to help those in need, such as the time she wrote to a priest friend asking him "to take up a collection for a family in dire need." Take the opportunity to participate in a collection for a worthy cause, such as a needy family in your own community.

- Bernadette was truly a prayer warrior. Make a concerted effort to take time out and pray for the intentions of at least one other person today.

- Make a conscious effort, perhaps starting small with just one class subject, to work to your greatest potential at your studies. In her writings, the saint said, "I would almost like to add this one resolution to yours so that you make the most of your time: 'I will also work very hard in class so that I may please Jesus.'"

- "I have just learned of the death of my father," said Saint Bernadette in her writings. "He died Saturday. Always have a great devotion for the agonizing heart of Jesus, for it is a consolation to know that we have prayed for those we love when we lose them and cannot be there. That is what I was doing on Saturday, praying for those in the final agony of death, never suspecting that I was praying for my poor father, who at that very moment was entering into eternity." Pause to pray for someone, whether known to you or anonymous, who is on the verge of death.

- Several movies have been made about the life of Saint Bernadette, among them *The Song of Bernadette* (1943), *Bernadette of Lourdes* (1960) and *Bernadette* (1988). Watch one or more of them and compare their telling of her story to the way you've pictured the events of Bernadette's life taking place.

# BLESSED CEFERINO NAMUNCURÁ

## LIGHTING OUR PATH TO SANCTITY

"We give thanks to the Lord for the extraordinary testimony of this young nineteen-year-old student, who, inspired by his devotion for the Eucharist and love for Christ, wanted to be a Salesian and a priest to show his fellow Mapuche the path to heaven. With his life, he lightens our path to sanctity, inviting us to love our brothers with the love with which God loves us."

—POPE BENEDICT XVI

**FEAST DAY**: AUGUST 26

When Ceferino Namuncurá was born on August 26, 1886, to Manuel Namuncurá and Rosario Burgos, he was the middle child in a family that would eventually total twelve kids. His father had high hopes for him to guide his people, but it's unlikely he realized just what sort of young leader his son would grow to be.

A little more than ten years before, John Bosco had started worldwide Salesian missions, with the first mission team being sent from Italy to Buenos Aires, Argentina. With Father John Cagliero, an Italian Salesian who was made vicar of Patagonia, at the helm, they spread the gospel until 1880, when they started work in Patagonia. One of the Salesian missionary priests in Patagonia, Father Dominic Milanesio, worked to promote the founding of a peace deal between the Mapuche native people and the Argentinian government, who had been sparring ceaselessly over land rights.

> **Blessed Ceferino** is also commonly referred to as Zepherin. Both translations of the name mean "gentle breeze."

The Mapuche lived in the South-Central areas of Chile and Southern Argentina, and the most important and tireless supporter of the Mapuche tribe's right to the land was Manuel Namuncurá. Manuel was not only a Mapuche chief, but the last Araucanian-speaking chief to refuse to submit to the European settlers' encroachment. Because of this, his people had suffered greatly for their cause. His own wife, as well as four of Ceferino's older siblings and about 2,000 other native peoples, had even been taken by the Argentine troops.

When Manuel had grown too weary of his people's suffering at the hands of war, he summoned Father Dominic Milanesio to his village. After welcoming the priest and sharing a meal with him, he proceeded to explain the sad plight of his people at the hands of Europeans, including battling for land rights against Argentinian General Roca; and that he was the last chief to keep fighting. The priest had come prepared to negotiate for a peaceful outcome. The government would offer Manuel and his Mapuche people 32,000 acres of land on a reservation along Chimay River in the pampas if they would move from the open plains, the military rank of colonel in the Argentine army, and he would be able to retain his role as chief. After spending a day in dance, worshiping the god Gneche, the people rested the next day and then surrendered to General Roca on May 5, 1882.

In December 1888, when Ceferino was two years old, Father Milanesio came back for his first visit in a while to Manuel and his people.

**Pope Saint Zephyrinus** served as pope from 198–217 during a time of severe Christian persecution in Rome. His feast is celebrated on December 20 of each year, commemorating his death on December 20, 217.

On Christmas Eve, Manuel, who had grown to trust and respect the priest, requested that the toddler be baptized that night. The child's baptismal name would be Ceferino, after Pope Zephyrinus.

Ceferino's young childhood was typical of Mapuche youth, as at the tender age of five he was already riding a pony and shooting with a bow and arrow. In 1894, however, the peace that his people had agreed to began to crumble. The treaty that had been established in 1882 between the Argentinian military and the Araucanians was changed to make more space for European settlers, and the native people were ordered to move further west, toward the rough terrain of the Alumine River. Manuel Namuncurá was understandably upset that the agreement had been broken and the military was forceably moving his people. Desperate, he began to rethink the peace deal and seek retaliation.

---

*"Serve God with joy!" —Father Dominic Milanesio's advice to Ceferino*

---

**Pope Saint Zephyrinus**

By the time Ceferino turned eleven in 1897, the boy was being taught the essentials of a chief's son. When Manuel made it known to the other Mapuche that he expected Ceferino to eventually follow in his footsteps to lead them, they were in agreement. As chief, Ceferino would have to be able to both serve the needs of the Mapuche and dialogue with the Argentine government—Manuel deemed that this would require formal education. That same year, Manuel and a few others traveled to accompany Ceferino to a military school in the city, venturing to the town of Zapala so they could all take a train to Buenos Aires. It was in Zapala that Ceferino saw other native people at the train station. They were in a large group of about 100 people loaded onto a freight car, and they were being pushed around and generally abused by Argentine soldiers. Bravely, Ceferino came to the defense of a man who had fallen down and was being beaten by a soldier.

When they got to the military school, Manuel requested that, as a colonel, his son be enrolled. Ceferino disliked the school environment, and who would in his place? Being the only native Argentinian there, he was bullied and homesick. When he started to become too thin and noticeably unwell, the school let Manuel know that his son was not making it and would have to be sent back to him. Not willing to give up his plan for Ceferino to receive formal schooling, Father Dominic suggested to Manuel that the Pius IX Salesian school in Buenos Aires might be just the thing.

At Pius IX, Ceferino immediately appreciated the more playful atmosphere, where fellow students welcomed and helped him with his Spanish. While the structured school life took an adjustment, he enjoyed the food and going to church, and wanted "...to study to be useful to my people." Before long, he wanted to be able to receive Communion, but needed some more religious education first. The big day came along at age twelve during his first spiritual retreat, when he received first Communion on September 8, 1898.

According to his superior at the school, "That day left a deep mark on his personality!" A year later, in 1899, Ceferino was confirmed. The sacraments inspired him to seriously strengthen in holiness. This manifested itself in

> **What do you remember** about your First Communion? What were you wearing? Who was there? Have you ever thanked the priest who celebrated the Mass for the occasion?

his training to become an altar server and a further dissatisfaction with his people's ritual sacrifices to gods, leading him to believe that, as chief, he would be able to lead them to the one, true God. He had a deep dislike of lying, and was so devoted to the Eucharist that he began to gaze into the hallway at the tabernacle light during class. His teacher thought he was just being inattentive to class and moved his seat, but he soon realized that Ceferino was justly distracted. When Manuel came to visit the Pius IX School, he gave his son a gift of ten pesos. So devoted was Ceferino to our Lady that he gave these pesos to the head of the school for flowers to adorn the Marian altar.

After attending the school for five years, Ceferino felt the call to become a Salesian and eventually go back to his people as their priest. Father John Cagliero, Don Bosco's original missionary to South America, sent him to Saint Francis de Sales seminary in Viedma, Argentina, a minor seminary with eleven students located on the coast southwest of Buenos Aires. Ceferino was the only native student and very impoverished. Since he was the son of a notorious warrior, with Manuel even being featured in his traditional Mapuche garb in the social studies book they used, the other students were curious about the differences between their cultures. These differences did not seem to concern Ceferino, except when his classmates made the occasional hurtful or even seemingly innocent embarrassing comment. For example, they questioned his father's failed war against the Argentine government and wondered aloud about the taste of human flesh. Even though he had difficulty with the Latin, which would be a necessary skill once he was a priest, he found that he had an expertise that many of his classmates

> *"The very life of Zepherin is like a 'parable' of this profound truth. Zepherin never forgot that he was a Mapuche: his supreme ideal was to be useful to his people. But encountering the Gospel made his fundamental aspiration grow in a new perspective: he came to ardently desire to be a Salesian, and a priest, 'to show' his brother Mapuche 'the way to heaven.'"*
>
> *—Tarcisio Cardinal Bertone, homily on the occasion of Blessed Ceferino's Beatification Mass, November 11, 2007*

**Tarcisio Cardinal Bertone**

"*Today, to magnify the Lord in Blessed Zepherin means also to actively and thankfully remember the ancient traditions of the proud and indomitable Mapuche People; and, at the same time, rediscover the fertility of the Gospel, which never destroys authentic values that a culture bears but assumes, purifies, and perfects them.*"

—*Tarcisio Cardinal Bertone, homily on the occasion of Blessed Ceferino's Beatification Mass, November 11, 2007*

did not and found himself teaching them how to hunt, fish, and ride horses, as well as acting as a witness to Christian young adulthood.

Now at seventeen years old, Ceferino was firm in his aspirations toward the priesthood. He naturally was found often in the chapel, whether serving Mass, working as a sacristan, or doing all sorts of maintenance and cleaning. According to a letter he sent back to students he had known at Pius IX, his former school, he felt "… so near my master in the Blessed Sacrament," and this showed in the little things, such as the extremely reverent manner in which he genuflected and the way in which he always made sure to look his best for church. Not only a leader in service to God, Ceferino also knew how to be a "gentle breeze" with his brother seminarians. He could charitably correct them in a way that was both humble and transformational, making them rethink their actions. For instance, on one occasion, some other teenagers came into the chapel talking. Ceferino, disturbed while at prayer, addressed them, saying, "I'm surprised to see that my friends have forgotten that this is God's house."

During the summer, Ceferino and the other seminarians worked at Saint Isidore's agricultural school in Patagonia, where he taught canoeing, would demonstrate card tricks, and greatly enjoyed archery—even crafting the bows and arrows himself. He made sure to balance hunting and his other outdoor pursuits with time in adoration and praying the rosary. It was this kind of prioritizing of worship to God and veneration of Mary that led Ceferino to organize a very special event.

Ceferino managed to prioritize prayer in the midst of other practices, such as hunting and canoeing. How well are you able to infuse prayer into the midst of other things you enjoy doing?

On September 24, 1903, the Feast of Our Lady of Mercy, Ceferino led a Marian procession around the school, complete with hymns, the recitation of the Rosary, an open-air Mass, and flowers all around the altar. As with the majority of his prayer life, he offered the honor "For my people, dear Queen," in order to secure the salvation of his own Mapuche brothers and sisters. The very next day, after coughing up blood, he realized he had contracted the disease known as Tuberculosis. At the time, there was no cure, but after a visit from Father John Cagliero, he went to the Salesian Saint Joseph's Hospital for care. According to the hospital chaplain, Ceferino "...rarely talked. We often thought he lived in continual prayer to God. He never gave signs of impatience or disgust. Grateful for any service, he smiled his thanks to all and obeyed every order given to him."

The following spring, in April 1904, Father Cagliero was made an archbishop and called to go to Rome. Thinking that the climate in Rome would be better for Ceferino, he got permission from Manuel to take Ceferino with him to recuperate and study. After one month of traveling from Buenos Aires to Rome, they arrived. He began his Italian seminary time in Turin, located in the north of Italy, and started there on July 19, 1904. Even though Ceferino was away from his homeland and immersed in a variety of activities, he managed to stay grounded and focused on getting better to become a priest to help his people. As a result, he constantly found time to spend with God. A priest who knew him while in Italy attested that, "Every time I looked for him, I found him praying before the picture of Mary Help of Christians." During the year he spent in Italy, Ceferino encountered more new and exciting adventures

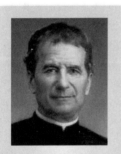

**John Bosco (1815-1888):** The Italian founder of the Salesians, Bosco died sixteen years before Ceferino's visit to Italy.

than many people do in the course of an entire lifetime. For example, he was invited by Bishop Cagliero to see John Bosco's incorrupt body moved to a different coffin. At an extremely popular mission exhibit in Turin to teach people about the different Catholic missions all over the world, Ceferino represented the Mapuche by wearing his native dress and educating people about the land and people of Patagonia. The queen of Italy was so impressed with him that she requested that he accompany her for the rest of the day. On September 29, 1904, the eighteen-year-old was given a private audience with Saint Pius X, where he shared his goal to become a priest and spread the gospel among his people.

**Pope Saint Pius X (1835–1914):** The son of a mailman, Pius X had a great devotion to Mary and warned against the errors of the modern age.

At the seminary in Turin, the cold climate caused Ceferino's tuberculosis symptoms to become more painful. For the next six months, he moved to Villa Sora, a seminary near Rome in Frascati, Italy. Even though he was struggling with sickness and learning his second, third, and fourth languages, he managed to keep up academically, becoming second in his class. But by March 1905, he was getting dramatically more ill. As a result, he suffered weight loss and a lack of energy, but the head of the seminary shared that "he was never impatient. He suffered, but he generously held on to his cross." At this time, he stayed in the school infirary before finally being moved to the Brothers of God Hospital in Rome. There, he spent time in prayer, reciting particularly the rosary, and finally received the sacrament of anointing of the sick before his death at six o'clock in the morning on May 11, 1905.

Ceferino's body was buried in Rome, but at the urging of his beloved Mapuche people, it was moved in 1924 back to his Patagonian homeland and buried at Fortin Mercedes Salesian school. In 1972, Ceferino Namuncurá was declared Venerable by Pope Paul VI, and on July 6, 2007, Pope Benedict XVI announced the approval of a miracle credited to his intercession, that of a thirty-three-year-old woman, Valeria Herrera, who was cured of uterine cancer in the year 2000.

## Catechetical Connection: Liturgy and Culture

The catechism tells us that the Catholic liturgy is for all people, in all times, and all places, and should be reflective of that reality.

> "The celebration of the liturgy, therefore, should correspond to the genius and culture of the different peoples. In order that the mystery of Christ be 'made known to all the nations...to bring about the obedience of faith,' it must be proclaimed, celebrated, and lived in all cultures in such a way that they themselves are not abolished by it, but redeemed and fulfilled" (*CCC* 1204).

The celebration of the liturgy should not oppress people of varying cultures but call them together in their uniqueness to worship God the Father. In celebrating the sacraments, Ceferino was not being less Mapuche, but realizing a fuller meaning of what it is to be a child of God, regardless of differences in cultural or geographical background.

**Polytheism:**
Belief in many gods

**Monotheism:**
Belief in one God

> "In the liturgy, above all that of the sacraments, there is an immutable part, a part that is divinely instituted and of which the Church is the guardian, and parts that can be changed, which the Church has the power and on occasion also the duty to adapt to the cultures of recently evangelized peoples" (*CCC* 1205).

In being baptized and raised as a Catholic, Ceferino was taking on the riches of the faith, as well as breaking with the traditional polytheistic worship of his Mapuche people.

*What sorts of differences have you noticed between varying Masses in your diocese?*

_____

_____

_____

*Have you ever been to a Mass celebrated in a different language or in a different country? If so, explain.*

_____

_____

_____

# PRAYER TO
# BLESSED CEFERINO NAMUNCURÁ

*"...We now address ourselves to your powerful intercession:*
*sustain our journey, so that we too can advance today*
*along the path of holiness, faithful to the teachings of Don Bosco.*
*"You have reached the heights of evangelical perfection,*
*fulfilling your duties well each day. You thus remind us that*
*holiness is not something exceptional, reserved for the elect few:*
*holiness is the common vocation of all the baptized,*
*and it is the demanding goal of ordinary Christian life.*
*"Help us to understand that, in the end, only one thing counts:*
*to be holy, as he, the Lord, is holy.*
*"...Guide us with your smiling gaze. Show us the way to heaven!*
*Accompany us all together to the encounter*
*with your friend Jesus."*
*Amen.*
*—Adapted from Cardinal Bertone's homily on the occasion of*
*Blessed Ceferino's Beatification Mass, November 11, 2007*

## MEMORY VERSE
### GALATIANS 3:28

"There is neither Jew nor Greek, there is neither slave
nor free person, there is not male and female;
for you are all one in Christ Jesus."

*Being a child of God is part of being baptized into Christ Jesus.
Do you remember your baptism? What have you been told?*

*Does the way that you live your faith and the work that you do adequately
reflect it?*

# Saintly Challenges

- As the son of a great Mapuche chief, Ceferino was proud of his heritage. Research your own family's ethnic background and make a unique family tree.

- Inspired by Ceferino's favorite sport, borrow or buy a bow and arrow and take lessons at an archery range. Make sure to use proper safety precautions.

- During the course of his schooling, Ceferino studied Spanish, Latin, and Italian. Work on your own proficiency in a second language. Also, converse with others who share a different cultural heritage than you and dialogue about what is unique, similar, and dissimilar. Share your stories.

- Not only was Ceferino active in the liturgy as an altar server, but he took it upon himself to clean the chapel. As part of your own efforts toward service in your parish community, volunteer to clean up or maintain some aspect of the parish grounds. You could rake leaves, mulch garden beds, pick up trash, or polish wooden pews. Inquire with your parish office to find out what needs to be accomplished!

- Ceferino used his ten pesos toward beautifying the Marian altar at school. Find a Marian statue in your own community that could use tending and pick up some flowers in honor of our Lady.

- Salesians are known for their outreach to youth, which includes sports, games, and even the card tricks, for which Ceferino is remembered. Here's an easy card trick you can try out on your friends:

  — Remove all the diamonds and even numbers from a deck of cards, and make sure the remaining cards are all facing the same way (this is easier if the backs of the cards have a unique pattern). This trick works better with fewer cards.

  — Ask someone to remove a card from the deck and memorize it. While he is looking at the card, rotate the deck 180 degrees.

  — Have him put the card back into the stack, and then shuffle as many times as you like. You can even have your friend shuffle.

  — Fan out the cards, and your friend's card will be easy to find. It'll be the one facing the opposite direction of the rest of the cards.

  — Repeat until your friend figures out how you did it.

# SAINT LUCY

## A LIGHT FOR CHRIST

"A pure offering is this...that one should visit widows, and comfort exiles, and help orphan children in their affliction."

—SAINT LUCY

**FEAST DAY**: DECEMBER 13

**PATRONAGE:** WRITERS, THE BLIND, THROAT INFECTIONS, SALESPERSONS, EPIDEMICS, ITALY

Saint Lucy was born around the year 283 to a Roman father and a mother who was probably of Greek descent. She is a holy woman remembered from early Church history. Her wealthy family lived in the city of Syracuse on the island of Sicily, a part of the Roman Empire in what is modern-day Italy. At the time of her birth, Diocletian was the ruler of the pagan Roman Empire. Her father died when she was around eleven years old, leaving her to be raised by a single mother, Eutychia.

> **"Lucy"** means "light," which is fitting because her December 13 feast day was the shortest day of the year, according to the Julian calendar, which was used during her lifetime.

Five years later, when Lucy was in her mid-teens, Eutychia began suffering from a hemorrhage and sought the help of doctors to find a cure. Four years later in 303, Lucy convinced Eutychia to go with her on a pilgrimage to the tomb of Saint Agatha in Catania, Sicily, to seek her intercession in the case of Eutychia's bleeding. It was this same year when the Emperor Diocletian began lashing out more fervently against the Christians in his empire through a series of edicts aimed at cutting them down.

> **Saint Lucy** was born only about thirty years after Saint Agatha's martyrdom in 251.

The pair took the journey to Catania and, upon arriving, went to Mass, where they heard the gospel story of the woman suffering from a hemorrhage who boldly touched Jesus' robe and was healed.

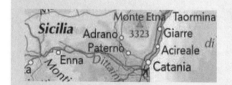

**Catania** lies about forty miles north of Syracuse on the island of Sicily.

**The story of the woman** afflicted with hemorrhaging, or bleeding, is found in three of the gospels: Matthew 9:20–22, Mark 5:25–34, and Luke 8:43–48. According to Mark's Gospel: "There was a woman afflicted with hemorrhages for twelve years. She had suffered greatly at the hands of many doctors and had spent all that she had. Yet she was not helped but only grew worse. She had heard about Jesus and came up behind him in the crowd and touched his cloak. She said, 'If I but touch his clothes, I shall be cured.' Immediately her flow of blood dried up. She felt in her body that she was healed of her affliction. Jesus, aware at once that power had gone out from him, turned around in the crowd and asked, 'Who has touched my clothes?' But his disciples said to him, 'You see how the crowd is pressing upon you, and yet you ask, 'Who touched me?' And he looked around to see who had done it. The woman, realizing what had happened to her, approached in fear and trembling. She fell down before Jesus and told him the whole truth. He said to her, 'Daughter, your faith has saved you. Go in peace and be cured of your affliction'" (Mark 5:25–34).

*In all three gospel accounts, Jesus tells the woman that her faith has saved her. How is this similar to Saint Lucy's experience?*

*What aspect(s) of your own life could use healing right now?*

Afterward, they cried and prayed at Saint Agatha's tomb until Lucy was so exhausted she fell asleep. It was then and there that the girl had a vision of Saint Agatha in heaven, who told Lucy her mother had been healed through Lucy's own faith: "My sister Lucy, true virgin of God, why prayest thou of me that which thou couldst thyself grant? Thy holy faith has helped thy mother, and lo! she is entirely healed by Christ; and even as this town is renowned through me, by Christ's favor, so shall Syracuse be renowned through thee, because thou didst yield thyself to Christ, in thy pure virginity, as a pleasant habitation."

After this mystical experience and Eutychia's miraculous cure, Lucy asked her mother to let her take the family's riches and the wealth that would have been her dowry and give it to the needy, living as a consecrated virgin. By doing so, Eutychia would be agreeing to not expect her daughter to marry or bear her any grandchildren. Eutychia asked Lucy that she wait until she herself had died to dispense with the family's riches, but Lucy reminded her mother that the wealth would be no use to her when she was already dead, saying, "listen to my counsel; thou canst take away nothing with thee out of this life,

**Burial of Saint Agatha**

and that which thou wilt give at death for the Lord's name thou wilt give because thou canst not take it away with thee. But give now, in thy time of health, to the true Saviour whatever thou intendest to dispose of at thy death." The mother gave in, and they proceeded in their almsgiving until they had given away almost everything.

But while her mother had agreed with Lucy's choice to consecrate her virginity to God, it was around the year 304 when the man she was betrothed to lost his temper. Having met Lucy's nurse and been told that Lucy had found someone better (Jesus!), he became angry, particularly because he felt cheated of Lucy's dowry and wealth. Women in Lucy's time were often considered property. To get back at her, he informed on her to Paschasius, the governor of Sicily. Paschasius then ordered her to sacrifice to the gods and worship them. She refused, saying, "A pure offering is this, and acceptable to God, that one should visit widows, and comfort exiles, and help orphan children in their affliction. I have not for three years been employed about any other deeds, but have offered these offerings to the living Lord. Now I desire verily to offer to him myself, because for some time I have had nothing to spend in his service." Lucy's words had no impact on him, so she responded that if he kept the laws of the empire's rulers, she should be able to keep God's law. Paschasius sentenced her to a life of prostitution, but then things started to get really crazy—by grace of the Holy Spirit, she was rooted so solidly to the ground that it was impossible for her captors to make her budge. Paschasius' servants tried to move her to no avail. They then put ropes on her hands and feet to drag her, but that didn't work either. Getting desperate, the court sorcerers were called on to use magic to move her. Finally, oxen were brought in to try and heave her away. Lucy retorted that ten thousand men wouldn't be able to make her move, further annoying Paschasius.

When it was clear a different tactic would be needed in order to kill her, flammable substances like tree pitch and extremely hot oil, as well as kindling and firewood, were placed all around Lucy's body in order to burn her alive. Again, the girl was kept safe through the saving power of God. It was then that Lucy proclaimed that she wanted her trials to demonstrate that they could not make her abandon Christ, and to give hope to other Christians in strife, that they might know that they could withstand the distress they might similarly be

**The seven women** mentioned during the eucharistic prayer at Mass include: Agatha, Agnes, Anastasia, Cecelia, Felicity, Lucy, and Perpetua.

undergoing: "I have obtained of Christ in prayer that this deadly fire may have no power upon me, that thou mayst be put to shame, and that it may dispel all fear of torture from believers and take away from unbelievers their [cruel] joy."

Finally, the blow of a sword dealt a lethal force through Lucy's throat. Before she died, Lucy received Communion from a priest and foretold that the Christian persecution would end, Paschasius would be disciplined for his actions, and the Emperor Diocletian and his henchman and co-emperor Maximilian's power would come to an end.

**Saint Lucy** is commonly depicted in art holding a plate with her eyeballs resting in it. Some legends refer to her eyes being pulled out of their sockets.

Today, the Basilica of Saint Lucy lies directly above the spot where the girl was so brutally tortured and martyred. She is remembered by name in the eucharistic prayer at Mass.

## Catechetical Connection: Almsgiving

After her mother Eutychia's miraculous recovery at the tomb of Saint Agatha, Saint Lucy pleaded with her that they might devote themselves to a life of almsgiving—giving charitable gifts to those in need. As the catechism states, almsgiving is a practice that allows the Christian to work with God toward a more equitable society.

**The corporal works of mercy:** Feed the hungry. Give drink to the thirsty. Shelter the homeless. Clothe the naked. Visit the sick and imprisoned. Bury the dead.

"The works of mercy are charitable actions by which we come to the aid of our neighbor in his spiritual and bodily necessities. Instructing, advising, consoling, comforting are spiritual works of mercy, as are forgiving and bearing wrongs patiently. The corporal works of mercy consist especially in feeding the hungry, sheltering the homeless, clothing the naked, visiting the sick and imprisoned, and burying the dead. Among all these, giving alms to the poor is one of the chief witnesses to fraternal charity: it is also a work of justice pleasing to God" (*CCC* 2447).

*With which of the corporal works of mercy do you have the most practice? How so?*

_____

_____

_____

_____

_____

_____

*Which corporal work of mercy are most outside of your comfort zone? Explain why.*

_____

_____

_____

_____

_____

# PRAYER TO SAINT LUCY

*Saint Lucy,*
*You made the ultimate sacrifice*
*in order to be faithful to your holy Spouse.*
*Help me to be true to Jesus every day,*
*with a willingness to freely suffer trials*
*big or small for love of him.*
*Light in me a desire and the strength to serve those in need,*
*and the fortitude to believe*
*that the Lord can truly heal all afflictions.*
*Amen.*

## MEMORY VERSE

### MARK 5:34

Like Lucy's mother Eutychia, the woman in the gospels who suffered from the hemorrhage faithfully sought out the healing power of the Lord.

"He said to her, 'Daughter, your faith has saved you. Go in peace and be cured of your affliction.'"

*What affliction within you—whether spiritual, physical, or mental—*
*would you like Jesus to work his curative power on?*

# *Saintly Challenges*

- In celebration of the light of Christ working in Saint Lucy's life, enjoy a bonfire or a fire in the fireplace.

  *Paschasius attempted to kill Saint Lucy by burning her alive. In remembrance of the miracle of her salvation from the fire, enjoy some roasted marshmallows, with the white of the marshmallow as a symbol of the girl's chastity and the stick you use to roast it with a reminder of the saint's final martyrdom at the hand of the sword.*

  *Remember to get your parent/guardian's approval and keep in mind any local ordinances involving bonfires or the use of permitted firewood. Also, avoid an outdoor fire if weather conditions are too dry and may pose an additional hazard.*

- In Scandinavian countries like Sweden, it is common for the oldest girl of the family to dress in a Saint Lucy costume, consisting of a white dress and a wreath with candles perched on her head, and serve her parents breakfast on December 13.

  *This weekend, surprise your family with a homemade breakfast.*

# SAINT GABRIEL OF THE SORROWFUL VIRGIN

## THE COURAGE OF HUMILITY

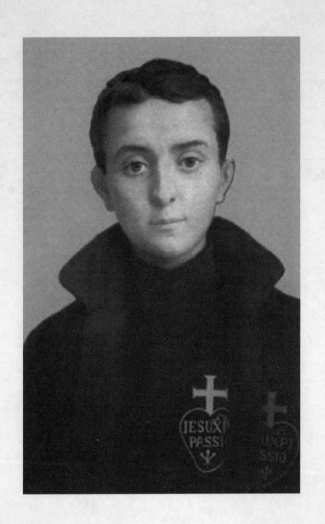

"In following Christ and imitating Mary,
we must have the courage of humility;
we must entrust ourselves humbly to the Lord,
because only in this way will we be able
to become docile instruments in his hands and
allow him to do great things in us.
The Lord worked great miracles in Mary and
in the Saints! I am thinking, for example,
of Francis of Assisi and Catherine of Siena,
Patrons of Italy. I am thinking also of splendid
young people like Saint Gemma Galgani,
Saint Gabriel of the Sorrowful Virgin,
Saint Louis Gonzaga, Saint Dominic Savio,
Saint Maria Goretti, born not far from here,
and the Blesseds, Pier Giorgio Frassati
and Alberto Marvelli."

—POPE BENEDICT XVI, SEPTEMBER 2, 2007, HOMILY ON THE OCCASION
OF THE AGORA OF ITALIAN YOUTH, PLAIN OF MONTORSO, ITALY

**FEAST DAY:** FEBRUARY 27

**PATRONAGE:** YOUTH, STUDENTS, SEMINARIANS, CLERICS

More than 700 years after Saint Francis of Assisi was baptized, another Saint Francis—Francesco Possenti—was baptized March 1, 1838, the same day Francis of Assisi was born. Both attended the same Italian church. Francesco Possenti's father, Sante, was a lawyer and local politician and his mother, Agnes, was an especially ardent Catholic who gave birth to fourteen children, ten of whom survived childhood. Francis was her eleventh child, but he was not destined to have the opportunity to get to know his mother for long. Francesco Possenti lived away from the family with a nurse for the first year of his life while his mom was sick. Sadly, she died less than four years after little Francesco was born. A governess aided the widower father in caring for the impulsive and active child and his siblings, and tutored them as well.

Sante was a good and devout Christian father who followed a daily schedule grounded in his love of God. He prayed for an hour each morning and attended daily Mass with his children before heading off to work, and then led his children in praying the rosary each night before taking time together to talk and relate their days. In addition to his devotional life, Sante practiced almsgiving to those less fortunate than himself, a practice that was to rub off on his children.

**Almsgiving:** The charitable giving of necessities—such as food, clothing, or money—to those in need.

What good and holy habits have you learned from your parent(s), guardian(s), or other relatives?

When he got to school age, Francesco attended a Christian Brothers elementary school. It was there that he was known to follow his father's example of charity by giving away his lunch to friends and needy classmates, including his beloved candy and sweets. He explained to his governess Pacifica that "…father wants us to be charitable; we ought not to despise the poor, for we don't know what we may one day be ourselves." While the boy was known to become very angry on occasion, he was also quick to seek forgiveness and reconcile and was generally acknowledged to have a true sense of integrity and honesty.

*What recurring situations in your life make you the most angry?*
*Toward which person in your life do you express the most anger?*
*How quickly are you able to reconcile, and have you even tried to reconcile?*

After finishing elementary school, he went on to a Jesuit high school until he was eighteen years old, where he was remembered for his exceptional intelligence and school honors. As Francesco himself admitted, however, his teenage years were spent as much navigating his social scene as they were with textbooks. While the young man continued to serve at Mass every morning and pray the rosary every night, he increasingly enjoyed dances, music, and putting on plays with friends. He also had a vain streak, being overly concerned with his looks, especially his clothing and hair.

*Is there any aspect(s) of your appearance that you're overly self-absorbed in?*

At one point, though, he got sick and made a promise to God that he would join a religious order if he got better, but seemingly forgot his promise when he recovered. Years later and sick again, this time with a swollen and infected throat that pointed to severe laryngitis, he became so ill one night that he was sure he would stop breathing and die. When he saw a picture of Blessed Andrew Bobola and put it to his throat—asking his intercession to God to heal him—he again made the promise to join a religious order.

**Mary Mother of Mercy**

Meanwhile, Francesco's seventeen-year-old life was suddenly thrown into chaos. Mary, his sister who had been like a second mother to him, contracted cholera in May 1855 and was the first in their city of Spoleto to die. The disease ravaged the people of the region until, in despair, it was decided that the icon of Mary Mother of Mercy would be used to bless all of Spoleto. Miraculously, it signaled the end of the city's cholera epidemic, and a Mass of thanksgiving was held on the feast of the Assumption to celebrate. As the Marian icon was processed throughout the cathedral, Francesco heard a voice saying, "Why! thou art not made for the world!…What art thou doing in the world?…Hasten, become a religious!…" This experience totally solidified his vocation to become a Passionist, and he met

**Blessed Andrew Bobola (1591–1657):** Polish Jesuit born into a noble family who worked with plague victims and was brutally tortured to death. Falling asleep, he awoke totally healed. It was then that he figured it was about time to live up to his promises. His first step was to approach the Jesuits, who agreed to accept him into the order, but he continued to put off the vocation. He was conflicted over whether he was truly called to the Jesuits or the Passionists, so he spent his time praying and held off from jumping into a decision.

with his confessor in August of 1856 before applying to the Passionists' provincial for admittance.

The next step, and possibly the most difficult, was to talk to his dad about his vocation. The eighteen-year-old shed tears as he spoke about the call he was feeling to religious life, but he wasn't prepared for his father's amused response. While one son, Aloyisius, was with the Dominicans and Henry was studying with the diocesan seminary, Sante thought that when it came to Francesco, his vain, fickle son must be experiencing a fleeting desire that would soon burn out. He thought that Francesco was not ready for the rigors of Passionist life and advised him to speak with his confessor, but when Francesco dramatically fell at his father's feet to beg for his approval, he begrudgingly said that he'd think it over.

On September 5, 1856, Francesco graduated from his Jesuit secondary school receiving a gold medal for high academic honors. He was dressed nicely, as according to his friend Bonaccia, "His clothes were unusually elegant; a matchless and richly folded shirt front adorned with jewels; bright buttons on his cuffs; a silk

> **Provincial:** The superior of the territory, known as a province, of a given religious order

cravat around his neck; his hair studiously parted; add to this picture his white kid gloves and patent-leather shoes...as he stood smiling and serene, facing his many friends and the distinguished audience, about to be the pleased spectators of his triumphs." What his friend and other classmates didn't know until the following day was that Francesco would be leaving for the trip of his life. By that time, under his father's guidance, he would be setting off with his brother, Aloysius, to visit the Shrine of Our Lady of Loreto and afterward visit their father's friend, the Vicar-General Father Caesar Acquacotta of Loreto.

> **Shrine of Our Lady of Loreto:** A church built around the traditional house where Mary lived with Jesus

> **Vicar-General:** The second-in-command after a diocesan bishop. From there, he and Aloysius would head to the Passionist novitiate in Morovalle.

September 6, 1856, found Francesco leaving for the shrine in Loreto, arriving on the night of September 7. The brothers went to the church at the shrine the morning of September 8 and greeted Father Acquacotta. Francesco then served Mass and met with Father Acquacotta to discuss his Passionist vocation, as Sante wanted Father Acquacotta to cross-examine Francesco's call to Passionist religious life in order to determine if it was true. If so, his father would agree to let him join the Passionists. Like Sante, however, the priest did not take him seriously, thinking Francesco was just being silly. Furthermore, he cited the teenager's weak health and the impact such a move would have on his father, encouraging Francesco to be a diocesan priest or layperson instead.

This was disheartening, but Aloyisius and Francesco continued on their road trip, stopping next in Morrovalle to visit the Franciscan monastery where his uncle served as the superior. It was here that Francesco's voyage starting looking up. His uncle believed his vocation to be genuine and would write Sante Possenti to let him know! He promptly went to church for confession, praying in thanks and asking for Mary to be his protectress.

The brothers were warmly welcomed when they visited their maternal grandparents' house on September 9, but Francesco was soon being teased and judged for wanting to join the Passionists. Francesco had to fight the same battle in defense of his vocation all over again, being told to think it over, that he wasn't physically strong enough, and to not say they didn't tell him so. To make things worse, at this point he hadn't yet received a reply from the Passionists telling him he would be admitted.

Nevertheless, the guys, accompanied by their Franciscan uncle, traveled on the very next day to the Passionist novitiate in Morrovalle. It was there that it was revealed that he actually had been accepted, and his father had intercepted the letter. A second letter had been sent out because Francesco had not yet replied, but they had left before it had arrived. By the time Francesco arrived to the Passionist novitiate, there was only one novice place remaining. Though the original plan was for Francis to visit and become acquainted with the Passionist lifestyle and then spend some time visiting his aunt in Montegiorgio before going back to the Franciscan monastery with his uncle, the young man decided he wanted to stay. When his brother checked on him the next day, he insisted on making his new life there if the Passionist community would still have him.

**Pilgrims Visiting the Shrine of Our Lady of Loretto, 18th Century**

After his admittance as a postulant, Francesco went on a ten-day retreat. He cried tears of joy upon taking the habit, later kneeling in the refectory and thanking the community for welcoming him in. In a letter to his father dated September 21, 1856, the eighteen-year-old recounted how he took the name Gabriel: "The Almighty had been calling me for a long time, whilst I ungratefully turned a deaf ear to his voice by enjoying the world and displeasing him; but his infinite mercy sweetly disposed all things, and today the feast of Our Lady of Sorrows, our Mother and Protector, I was clothed in the holy habit, taking the name of Confrater Gabriel, of the Seven Dolors." Confrater Gabriel of the Seven Dolors, otherwise known as Brother Gabriel of the Sorrowful Virgin, was not just taking on a new style of clothing and name, but an entirely new lifestyle.

**Refectory:** A monastery dining room

*Saint Gabriel seemed to his family and peers as an unlikely candidate for the priesthood. Is there a priest or religious in your life who surprised his or her family upon announcing he or she would be pursuing a religious vocation?*

This transition is apparent in a letter written to a friend that states, "...I protest that whatever evil I may have spoken about anyone, I now unsay it, and beg of you to forget it all and to pray for me that God may forgive me likewise." Speaking of letters, generally, the men of his community wrote home three to four times a year.

On Tuesday, September 22, 1857, Gabriel made vows to the Passionist order, proclaiming, "Through the grace of God, and the protection of Our Lady of Sorrows, and to my unspeakable joy, my desires have been fulfilled, and I have made my holy profession. Such a grace can never be valued adequately...."

Because it is the Passionist custom to move around to study, along with his spiritual director and confessor Father Norbert, he made his way to Pievetorina, Italy, to study privately for five months before studying for another year with newly professed Passionists. He then moved to a monastery in Naples, Italy.

While Saint Gabriel didn't outwardly seem much different from his brother Passionists, it was the sheer magnitude of his interior life that was bewildering. According to Father Norbert, who acted as Gabriel's spiritual director until the end of his life, the saint was a hard worker, never giving up "...in his spiritual progress whether on account of aridity, weariness or temptation; whether he had the consolation of sensible devotion or not. He ever acted with energy of soul, greatness and generosity of mind, never neglecting himself inadvertently in anything, ever growing in the

> **"He is a youth of strong purpose, as fervent and virtuous as can be desired, and if he so continues, as we have every reason to hope, he will really become a saint."**
>
> —Saint Gabriel's Novice Vice-Master Father Norbert

perfection of his interior dispositions." As a result, he stayed focused on God, including his work as a Passionist, academics, and spiritual endeavors, and avoided unnecessary musings and talking.

**One method** that Saint Gabriel used for accelerating his sanctity was writing down and living by about forty resolutions that later came into the Passionists' possession. Some of these include:

- "I will never excuse myself when I am corrected or blamed nor even resent anything interiorly; much less throw the blame on others."

- "Every morning and evening I will practice some act of humility and endeavor gradually to increase their number."

- "I will rejoice in the good done by others, and will account it a fault to feel any sentiment of envy; neither will I allow myself to be interested in vain things."

- "I will not break silence without real necessity."

- "I will be punctual. I will obey the sound of the bell as if it were the very voice of God."

- "I will not speak of the faults of others, even if everybody knows them already; nor will I show any sign of disesteem for them, either in their presence or behind their back. I will speak of every one with great regard."

- "I will try not to provoke anybody by using sharp words, nor will I speak in such a way as to make one feel bad."

- "I will be contented with what is served, without ever complaining either in word or thought...."

*Many of Saint Gabriel's resolutions are ones that would be practical and good even for people who aren't living as vowed religious, such as those in the Passionist community. Add a resolution of your own that would be helpful to live by:*

In terms of living a virtuous life, Gabriel, who had once been so self-centered when it came to everything from the way he dressed to the recreation he sought, daily practiced humble charity, which was in keeping with the Passionist order's vow of poverty. He strove not to overdo his food intake, saving the best of his dinner for those in need, and reminding his father to care for the poor, such as when he wrote to him saying, "One of the greatest consolations at the hour of death will be to remember that you never sent the poor away from your door empty-handed." No longer having any private property, he kept a modest demeanor, seeking out used clothing and other necessary articles, and he never bragged about how important his family and friends out in the world were. Instead, he favored spending time with people who were unpopular or looked down upon.

> "Considering the circumstances of Confrater Gabriel's life as a secular, to behold him now in religion, and even from the very beginning, so detached from all things, so humble, obedient, reserved and delicate of conscience, must necessarily impress one with the conviction that he set about the reformation of himself…."
>
> —Father Bernard

Likewise, he was known for helping anyone in any way possible, even taking on his brother Passionists' punishments when they had committed wrongdoings.

Saint Gabriel seemed to throw all the energy he had previously spent on going to parties and making sure he looked just right into his new focus on religious observance. Paying special attention to always making sure he was on time, following the Passionists' daily schedule, he served as a sacristan and spent five to six hours a day in front of the tasiyacle in adoration, with his Passionist brothers recalling that, in order to get his attention, he'd literally have to be jostled to snap out of his prayer time. His major religious devotions were to Christ's passion and Mary's sorrow in witnessing that passion. He followed the rule by keeping his eyes

**Saint Paul of the Cross**

and heart frequently inclined to meditation on a crucifix, keeping one ever on his bedside table. For Mary, he shared in the troubles she had, as indicated by his name in religious life, "of the Sorrowful Virgin," as well as the Passionist rule, which states, "They

should honor with due devotion, the Blessed Mary Mother of God, ever Virgin; have her for chief patroness, constantly commemorate the most bitter sorrows which she suffered in the Passion and death of her Son, and promote veneration both by word and by example." In 1861, after five years of seeking permission from a spiritual director, he took a vow devoting himself to her. Saint Gabriel had other special devotions including an appreciation for Saint Joseph, remembering him especially on Wednesdays, and that of Saint Francis of Assisi, as they were both born and baptized in Assisi. The saints were such an important part of Gabriel's life of faith that he made a litany (a prayerful list) of all the saints especially important to him.

*If you were to write your own litany of saints, list three you would choose:*

_____

_____

_____

_____

Even with the joy of religious life, things weren't always easy. His companions sometimes noticed Gabriel's temper appear on his face,

but he worked very hard not to give in to anger. While he persevered in his prayer life, he was also frequently dealt temptations against whatever he might be praying about, causing him to have doubts about God. Additionally, his health was not good.

While he was fairly healthy during the first four years of religious life, he started to show signs of wearing down, but he patiently dealt with discomforts and kept to the communal routine as much as he was allowed, even though his superiors encouraged him to abstain from fasting and night prayer (matins). While ill he was quite upbeat and did not fear death, even though he was very weak by the end of 1861 until mid-February 1862. When hemorrhaging began, the twenty-five-year-old received viaticum, his last holy Communion, requesting to receive it on his knees (but was refused). During the next nine days, he was remarkably cheerful considering he was so mortally sick with tuberculosis. He received the anointing of the sick and, realizing the end was near, asked his spiritual director to burn his spiritual journal. By the evening of February 26, he suffered various temptations, including those toward presumption (pridefully assuming one's admittance into heaven) and against chastity.

**Saint Gabriel** was buried according to the Passionist rule:

- the body in a habit with profession
- cross in hands held over the heart
- the body laying on board in its own cell
- ashes put on the head, with the head laying on bricks
- later, taken to the church

The next morning, he asked for absolution, but his spiritual director Father Norbert didn't believe that it was time for his death. Requesting a picture of Our Lady of Sorrows to meditate upon, he prayed to Jesus, Mary, and Joseph. When his breathing slowed, the community was called for and he died, there at the Passionist retreat of the Immaculate Virgin at Isola de Gran Sasso, Italy. He had been a Passionist for a little over five and a half years.

On the morning of February 28, 1862, Saint Gabriel's funeral was celebrated, and he was buried in a vault. A year later, due to political upheaval, the Passionists were forced to leave Isola, but in 1891, Gabriel's Passionist superiors started the process toward beatification and canonization. On October 17, 1892, the bishop of Penne sent a group to Gabriel's burial spot to inspect the remains, but when the group arrived, they amazingly found hundreds of residents of Isola there to contest the removal of Gabriel's body, though they had not told anyone they were coming. Four thousand people gathered to ensure the remains were not taken from the church on October 18, 1892, thirty years after his death. Of that number, 200 to 300 people crammed into the church to watch the proceedings. Gabriel's bones, leather belt, and the Passionist symbol from his habit had withstood the test of time on his remains. His bones were placed on a white cloth, put in the casket with bishop's seal on it, and the crowd was allowed to gather around it, placing wreaths and flowers upon the casket, before it was placed in a burial vault in the chapel of Saint Paul of the Cross.

> *"That Confrater Gabriel practiced all manner of virtues in a heroic degree is clear from the unanimous testimony of all the witnesses, so that he could be held up as an excellent model of the highest perfection. All admired his promptitude and ease in the practice of virtue, and spoke of him as a saint. It was evident that he kept before his eyes and in his heart the examples of Christ and His saints, whom he ever strove to imitate with the greatest earnestness. He was ever advancing in holiness, no matter what the hindrance might be; like a valiant soldier (whose courage is tried on the field of battle) the harder the struggle, the more brightly did his perfection shine forth, so that all his acts of virtue might truly be called heroic. In this holy exercise he persevered until death, and no one was ever found to contest his claim to exalted virtue."*
>
> —Roman Commission's report on Saint Gabriel

Near the end of 1894, beatification and canonization were being discussed more seriously. Investigators journeyed to places where Gabriel had lived to get interviews from people who had known him, such as siblings, college friends, fellow religious, his confessor, and spiritual director. By June 4, 1895, his letters and other writings had been considered and were confirmed to be true, without faulty teachings. The next year, on July 7, 1896, his cause was formally opened. In May 1905, Pope Pius X announced Gabriel had lived the virtues heroically, especially mentioning faith, hope, charity, prudence, jus-

**Theological virtues:** faith, hope, and charity

**Cardinal virtues:** prudence, justice, fortitude, and temperance

tice, fortitude, and temperance; on January 26, 1908, his miracles were approved. That May 31, during the month we honor Mary, he was beatified in Saint Peter's in Rome, with 30,000 people in attendance. His canonization came about May 13, 1920, under the pontificate of Pope Benedict XV.

## THE SEVEN SORROWS OF MARY

**The Seven Sorrows of Mary are:**

1. Simeon's prophecy to Mary: *"Behold, this child is destined for the fall and rise of many in Israel, and to be a sign that will be contradicted (and you yourself a sword will pierce) so that the thoughts of many hearts may be revealed"* Luke 2:34–35.

2. Mary, Joseph, and Jesus' flight to Egypt

3. Twelve-year-old Jesus missing in the Temple in Jerusalem

4. The Mother-Son reunion during Jesus' climb to Calvary

**The feast of Our Lady of Sorrows is September 15.**

5. Mary's mourning at the foot of the cross

6. Jesus taken down from the cross

7. Jesus' burial in the tomb

"O! how pleasant it is to lay one's self down to rest, with the consciousness of having served God (however unworthily) during the whole day!"

—*Saint Gabriel of Our Lady of Sorrows*

## Catechetical Connection: Communion with Mary

"Mary is the perfect Orans (pray-er), a figure of the Church. When we pray to her, we are adhering with her to the plan of the Father, who sends his Son to save all men. Like the beloved disciple we welcome Jesus' mother into our homes, for she has become the mother of all the living. We can pray with and to her. The prayer of the Church is sustained by the prayer of Mary and united with it in hope" (*CCC* 2679).

We know that Saint Gabriel had a great devotion to our Lady's Seven Sorrows, going so far as to take on her title as part of his own name. As the catechism points out, Mary is both a model of an awesome prayer life as well as an intercessor of prayers to the Father in heaven. She said it best at Cana with, "Do whatever he tells you" (John 2:5). When we align our life with Mary's, we draw ourselves close to the will of her Son.

# PRAYER
## FROM THE *STABAT MATER DOLOROSA*

Pray these verses from the ancient *Stabat Mater Dolorosa* hymn, Latin for "The Sorrowful Mother Stood," and recall the great anguish Mary felt for her Son and Messiah during his passion and death on the cross. The rest of the hymn can be found in the appendix.

*Mary, fount of love's devotion,*
*Let me share with true emotion*
*All the sorrow you endured.*
*Virgin, ever interceding,*
*Hear me in my fervent pleading:*
*Fire me with your love of Christ.*
*Mother, may this prayer be granted:*
*That Christ's love may be implanted*
*In the depths of my poor soul.*
*Amen.*

## MEMORY VERSE
### MATTHEW 25:40

"And the king will say to them in reply,
'Amen, I say to you, whatever you did for one of these
least brothers of mine, you did for me.'"

*Saint Gabriel's love for the poor, including the socially poor, those whom other people avoided, was one of his greatest character traits.*

*Recount a time when you reached out to someone who was lonely or unpopular.*

# Saintly Challenges

- As part of his devotion to Mary, Saint Gabriel liked reading Saint Alphonsus Liguori's *The Glories of Mary*. Pick up your own copy of this classic work by visiting liguori.org or by calling 800-325-9521.

  *The Passionist rule states, "Let the meditations generally be about the divine attributes and perfections, and also about the mysteries of the life, passion, and death of our Lord Jesus Christ, from which all religious perfection and sanctity takes its rule and increase."*

- Using the stations of the cross, spend some time in prayer reflecting on Christ's passion.

- Pray the Litany of Our Lady of Sorrows found in the appendix. Better yet, since it has leader and response parts, pray it with an entire group of people.

- As part of Saint Gabriel's daily routine, he walked the monastery grounds for half an hour a day. Make it a priority to take a reflective half-hour walk today.

- Take some time to meditate on the *Stabat Mater Dolorosa* or find a sung version and listen to it either in English or Latin.

# BLESSED
# LAURA VICUÑA

## FAITH AND PIETY

"Faith and piety, so deeply rooted in the
Chilean soul, have been most fruitful,
even producing...the blessed servants of God
like Blessed Laura Vicuña...."

—POPE JOHN PAUL II, JUNE 18, 2001, ADDRESS OF THE HOLY FATHER
TO THE NEW AMBASSADOR OF CHILE TO THE HOLY SEE

**FEAST DAY:** JANUARY 22

**PATRONAGE:** ABUSE VICTIMS, LOSS OF PARENTS,
MARTYRS, INCEST VICTIMS, ARGENTINA

On April 5, 1891, Laura Vicuña was born in civil war-torn Chile to José Vicuña, a military man, and his wife, Mercedes. Because the country was enmeshed in civil war, Laura was not baptized until May 24. Shortly afterward, due to a Vicuña relative becoming politically unpopular and controversial, Laura's father was forced to move them from the capital city of Santiago southward to Temuco, Chile (located in the center of the country), for the safety of his young family. Little Laura was sickly, however at about a year and a half old she started to get better. It was not long after this that her sister, Julia, was also born, but the family was forever changed and uprooted again when José died and Mercedes decided it was necessary to move and find work to support her girls.

*Have you ever been in a situation where you didn't know anyone?*
*How did it feel to be the new person?*

Without a clear sense of where they were headed, the trio traveled to Norquin, Chile, where they rested up for some days before making their way to Las Lajas, Argentina. It was in Las Lajas that the Salesian missionaries who served the area recommended a newly founded Salesian Sisters' school in Junin de los Andes, Argentina. On January 21, 1900, Mercedes and the girls moved themselves and their belongings to Quilquihue, Argentina, a ranching community located fifteen miles from the girls' new boarding school. Mercedes would live in the community, full of rough and often vulgar ranchers, while the girls would receive the good education that Mercedes so desperately wanted for them. The sisters differed in how they reacted to the news. While the fun-loving Laura was excited at the prospect of the school, Julia was only six and understandably didn't want to leave her mother.

*What is your view on school? Do you enjoy taking classes or do you count down the minutes until lunch? What is your favorite subject?*

_____

_____

_____

_____

_____

Even though Laura had had little to no previous religious education, when she entered the school's Our Lady of Snows chapel, "...she looked at 'Jesus' little house,' as she called the tabernacle, and, when she was told that Jesus lived there, she blew him a kiss and promised to come back often." She started spiritual reading, a practice she would continue while on vacations at home, and by the spring of 1901, she was going to confession every week, in order to build up her spiritual strength and be stainless when she would receive Christ at her first Communion.

*What do you remember about your first confession?*
*When was the last time you went?*

_____

_____

_____

_____

Laura was very obedient to the sisters and helpful in her school community, but the excitement of her impending first Communion made Laura aspire to new heights, saying, "You will see how good I'll be! Nobody will ever have to complain about me!" The day of her first Communion finally came on June 2, 1901, and Mercedes came to see eleven-year-old Laura on her special day. Sadly, while Laura was growing in spiritual wisdom and maturity, Mercedes, living on her own in Quilquihue, had moved in with rancher Manuel Mora, a man who considered her to be his property to do with as he saw fit. While Laura could not quite understand why she felt the situation was wrong, she nonetheless tried to get her mother to come live with her. In reply, Mercedes simply asked for her prayers, but that Christmas she would be put to the test.

When Christmas vacation came, Laura's mother wanted the girls to come to the home she was living in with Manuel Mora and spend the break with her. Laura was torn. She loved her mother, but the arrangement back at her mother's home didn't thrill her. Nevertheless, the Salesian Sisters encouraged her to do what her mother asked of her.

Even though it turned out that she didn't see Mora that much, and he seemed to try to be less vulgar than she had remembered him, Mercedes was totally and scarily subservient to him. Frightened of the man and doing anything he asked of her, she was even scared to let him know they prayed, asking the girls to hide their prayer life.

The Salesian Sisters of Saint John Bosco, or Daughters of Mary Help of Christians, are the sister order of the Salesians of Don Bosco.

Yet it was Manuel Mora's decision to host the town dance, which really escalated things in the house.

Laura decided she didn't want to be around Manuel's drunk friends and employees from the ranching community, so she decided to hide in a dog shed behind the main house all night. It turned out that Manuel was furious that she wouldn't attend, finding her behavior to be offensive. When she came in to help her mother clean up and found Mercedes crying, she knew trouble was lurking. At lunch, Manuel blew up at Laura, telling her he wouldn't pay her school tuition any longer. When Mercedes sought advice from their sensible neighbor, Felicita Espinosa, she kindly went and advocated for Laura to the Salesian sisters. In turn, the sisters promised that they would take Laura back regardless of her ability to pay the tuition. Fortunately, Laura did not have to see Manuel Mora much for the rest of her break. He was busy tending to the ranch, and by March, Laura headed back to Junin to live with the Salesian sisters, while Julia stayed in Quilquihue to keep Mercedes company.

*Recount a time when you chose not to participate in a social situation that you knew would not be good for you. How did others react?*

It was during this period that Laura was being catechized in preparation for her Confirmation. She was very helpful with household chores, even foregoing leisure time to assist the sisters with anything they might need. She looked out for the neediest girls at school and gave up her own clothing, candy, and food, and protected them from bullying, such as those who would make fun of them because of their

**Bishop John Cagliero**

clothing. She even cared for those elsewhere who were less fortunate, giving her allowance money to missionary groups.

When Bishop John Cagliero came to Junin on March 6, 1902, to found mission chapels elsewhere in the Patagonia region, a Mass was celebrated in the school's chapel. From Palm Sunday through Holy Week, he preached at a parish mission in Junin, and Mercedes, Julia, and their neighbor Felicita Espinosa, along with crowds of people from all over the area, came for the special event. This was a time of great spiritual fervor for Laura, culminating in Easter, the day she was confirmed. Supported by her confirmation sponsor, Felicita, the only thing missing was her ability to celebrate the sacraments with her mother. Because of her relationship with Manuel

Mora, Mercedes missed Communion, deeply grieving Laura. On Easter Monday, Mercedes, Julia, and Felicita headed back to Quilquihue, but Laura had an idea brewing.

Bishop Cagliero would be presiding over a postulant receiving the sisters' veil and a sister taking vows, and Laura requested that she be allowed to join the Salesians, especially wanting to give herself as a gift to God on behalf of her mother's soul. When the bishop told her that eleven years old was too young to become a sister, advising her to continue to pray, she sought out Father Louis Pedemonte, her confessor. Being obedient to the bishop's reply, Laura requested that she be allowed to make a private vow to religious life. The priest was concerned about the gravity of such a promise, but upon making sure she would do her very best to keep it if allowed to, he

**Mary Help of Christians**

agreed that promises of poverty, chastity, and obedience would be all right, as long as she agreed that they would be privately kept, temporarily, and she would be able to reaffirm them if she wished on great holy days. Laura made her private vows in the Our Lady of Snows chapel.

*Which of the promises that Laura made—those of poverty, chastity, and obedience—would be the most difficult for you to keep? Why?*

That spring, her faith life rose to new heights. On May 24, 1902, at a school feast day honoring Mary Help of Christians, Laura offered a special spiritual offering to Mary. With Mercedes and Julia in attendance, Laura read an original piece she had written for Mary in front of the whole Junin community. Afterward, she unsuccessfully begged her mother and sister to move away from Manuel Mora to Junin.

During June 1902, Laura got sick and was sent to recuperate in bed, having to intermittently take cold baths as a remedy. Facing a very cold Southern Hemisphere winter and tempted to believe God did not hear her prayers, she started to feel alone and have no spiritual consolation. Nevertheless, she persevered, staying in Junin with the sisters and helping them with the orphans' religious education for the community children.

*What kinds of volunteer work are you involved in?*
*If you aren't currently involved in any, why not?*

_____

_____

_____

_____

_____

While Laura was an average student, she was amazing in terms of the depth of her spiritual life. With the other girls mocking her devotion, calling her "Jesus' slave," living her life for Christ was already by no means easy. Yet by 1903, Laura was continuing to grow in fortitude, so much so that during the Easter season, she made a very brave

and serious decision. Inspired by the gospel imagery of the Good Shepherd laying down his life for his sheep, she asked her confessor to allow her to literally lay down her own life for that of her mother's. While her confessor gave his consent for her to make the serious offering of her very self to God for her mother's conversion, she humbly kept the decision a secret.

*"She applied herself to prayer with such earnestness that she was not even aware of things about her. More than once we had to remind her that it was time to leave the chapel."* —*Sister Superior Angela Piaia*

Shortly thereafter, Laura again got sick and was getting worse very quickly. It was so serious that a doctor was called in, but she was given medications and eventually felt well enough to be able to be up and around. However, by the time Mercedes visited for the annual May devotions, she realized that Laura was not well and went back to Manuel Mora's worried for her daughter. By July, torrential rains caused the school to close, and the students and Salesian sisters sought shelter in a nearby community. When they were resituated back at school, Mercedes came to make sure Laura was OK, but by that time Laura's health had declined and Mercedes wanted her to come home immediately. She finally agreed with the sisters that they could wait until September and see if Laura got better.

When September rolled around and her mother came from Quilquihue for her, Laura did not want to leave the Salesians but dutifully packed her things. Even though she was not troubled by Manuel Mora at the ranch and she enjoyed taking walks and just getting to spend time with her mother and sister, Laura deeply missed the sisters and their chapel. As a result, Mercedes decided to move their small family to Junin, and finally fulfilled Laura's wish that she leave Manuel Mora.

While their new life together involved daily Mass, reading, and praying together, Laura's sickness continued and Manuel stalked and harassed the family, claiming Mercedes was his to do with as he pleased and she must come back to him or else. Not only was Laura upset to see her mother continuing to be treated as an object by the man, but Mercedes was still far from God, as signified by her not receiving Communion.

On January 14, 1904, thirteen-year-old Laura was with her mother in their family home when a drunk Manuel broke in holding a horsewhip. Threatened, Mercedes told Laura to run away, but when she did

so, Laura fell into the road and Manuel caught up with her, merciless-
ly whipping her face, shoulders, and back in the middle of the street.
Kicking and yelling expletives at her, he picked up her body before the
neighbors heard Mercedes and Julia screaming and came after him.
He then dropped Laura to the ground and the kindly Felicita Espinosa
tended to her while he fled back to his ranch on horseback. Laura tried
to pray all the while Felicita had her bathed, had oils put on her, and
sent for a priest. When Laura spoke to the priest, she unmaliciously
said, "I forgive him, Father. I bear him no grudge." Nevertheless, Laura
became weaker and asked for the community's prayers.

By January 17, Laura asked Mercedes for the chaplain from school,
Father Crestanello, who had served as her spiritual director. She wanted
to go to the sacrament of reconciliation, believing that death was im-
minent. With great faith, Laura let him know, "Father, this pain is ter-
rible...yet the grace that gives me hope is great!" Laura was in severe
pain, finding it difficult to breathe, and not sleeping nor eating. Grace
was all Laura had, besides her family, as the priest had to leave for
Santiago, Chile, with the Salesian sister superior. She would have to be
brave to handle the tuberculosis symptoms she was suffering coupled
with her physical abuse at the hands of Manuel Mora.

On Friday, January 22, Communion was brought to Laura, and
she received the anointing of the sick. It was then that she confided
to Mercedes that she was offering up her life for the salvation of her
mother's. Mercedes promised that she was finished with Manuel Mora
forever, even swearing in front of the priest that she would get right
with God and come back to the sacraments. That evening at 6 p.m.,
Laura died repeating the names of Jesus, Mary, and Joseph while the
Angelus bells rang.

The whole community came to view the body of the teenage girl in
a white dress and veil, holding a rosary and prayer book. That night,
Mercedes received the sacrament of reconciliation and received communion at Laura's funeral Mass the next day. She was humbly open about
the fact that Laura had sacrificed her own life for that of her mother.

Like Laura's Savior, she was buried in a borrowed tomb, that of an
above-ground burial hut given by a neighbor. As word of Laura's devo-

tion spread, the place quickly became a center of popular devotion, but that did not stop her abuser, Manuel Mora, from continuing to haunt the Vicuñas. He came back while Mercedes was with friends, again bringing a whip and demanding Mercedes come back to him. When she refused, he threatened to kill her and only left when he feared the neighbors would come after him. This happened over and over again for the next few years, and Mercedes moved in with one of the town families while Julia lived with the Salesian sisters. Manuel died three years after assaulting Laura, in a fight with other ranchers, while Mercedes moved back to Chile and got married again, living there until her death in 1929.

In 1954, the year Laura's diocese's bishop opened her cause for beatification and canonization, the Argentinian government approved the Salesian Sisters' plans to transfer Laura's body from her grass and mud hut tomb to a grave at the school she had loved so much.

On September 3, 1988, Pope John Paul II declared Laura Vicuña Blessed.

### Catechetical Connection: Cohabitation

When Laura was preparing for the sacrament of confirmation, her class also spent time learning about the sacrament of marriage. Laura literally fainted, as for the first time since living with the sisters, she realized just how wrong it was for her mother to be living with Manuel Mora in a sexual relationship outside the bonds of marriage. She was upset that her mother was cutting herself off from God through her mortal sin, and therefore unable to receive Communion. It was then that Laura dedicated herself to making amends for her mother's misdeeds through spiritual atonement.

According to Salesian Mother Superior Angela Piaia, "This sad realization (that it was wrong of her mother to be living with Manuel Mora) was her constant martyrdom, the one subject of her prayers and mortifications which she offered in reparation and in an endless plea for pity. For a soul such as Laura's aspiring to the purity of the angels, finding no sacrifice too great, no humiliation too harsh to keep her classmates from sin—she would gladly have died rather than submit to sin—it was a real torture for her to feel that her mother might have withdrawn herself from God."

"In a so-called free union, a man and a woman refuse to give juridical and public form to a liaison involving sexual intimacy. The expression "free union" is fallacious: what can "union" mean when the partners make no commitment to one another, each exhibiting a lack of trust in the other, in himself, or in the future?

"The expression covers a number of different situations: concubinage, rejection of marriage as such, or inability to make long-term commitments. All these situations offend against the dignity of marriage; they destroy the very idea of the family; they weaken the sense of fidelity. They are contrary to the moral law. The sexual act must take place exclusively within marriage. Outside of marriage it always constitutes a grave sin and excludes one from sacramental communion" (CCC 2390).

**Fallacious:** An inaccurate view

*Recall an instance when you had difficulty making a commitment to something you knew was worthwhile.*

# PRAYER OF LAURA VICUÑA

*Oh Jesus, I want to love and serve you all my life,*
*and so I offer you my soul, my heart, and all that I am.*
*I want to die before ever offending you by sin;*
*and therefore I want to mortify myself*
*in everything that might take me away from you.*
*I promise to do all I can, at the cost of any sacrifice,*
*to make you known and loved;*
*to make up to you for all the offenses*
*you receive every day from people,*
*especially my own family.*
*My God, give me a life of love,*
*of satisfaction, of sacrifice.*
*Amen.*

## MEMORY VERSE
### JOHN 10:14–15

"I am the good shepherd, and I know mine and mine
know me, just as the Father knows me and I know the
Father; and I will lay down my life for the sheep."

*Briefly relate the story of someone else you have heard of who risked or gave*
*up his or her life for that of someone else.*

---

"Be good to mama, don't give her trouble,
respect her always. Don't ever leave her,
even if later on you will have a family of your own.
Don't look down upon the poor,
but be kind to them.
Love our Lord and the Blessed Virgin.
Pray every day to your guardian angel
to keep you from sin. Don't forget, Julia.
We will be together in heaven."

—*Blessed Laura's last words to her sister, Julia*

# Saintly Challenges

- Among the items on Blessed Laura's desk at school was an image of the Sacred Heart of Jesus. Find a holy image of Christ to keep among your school things and help you recall his love for you.

- Blessed Laura shared with a friend that she sometimes had to pinch herself in order to stay awake at Mass. This week, make an extra effort to be alert at Mass, not letting your mind wander from the amazing gifts of the Word and the Eucharist.

- According to the Salesian mother superior who knew and loved her, "Laura was always obedient in big things and small, in things she liked and things she did not care for. She did not only the things the sisters asked her to do, but often enough she obeyed the wishes of her schoolmates." Today, do something your parent or guardian asks of you (such as taking out the trash, going to bed, turning off the television, clearing your plate from the table…) the first time, instead of making him or her repeat it.

- One thing Blessed Laura was known for was being very neat and orderly. If you struggle with being organized, try keeping your clothes off your bedroom floor all this week.

- Blessed Laura was very humble, which helped her in being willing to admit when she was at fault. The next time you are in the wrong, freely admit it and ask for pardon.

- Try praying the Angelus (found in the appendix) at 6 a.m., noon, or 6 p.m. today or tomorrow, or pray it at all three times.

# THE ANGELUS

The Angel of the Lord declared unto Mary:

**R.** And she conceived of the Holy Spirit.

Hail Mary, full of grace, the Lord is with thee; blessed art thou among women and blessed is the fruit of thy womb, Jesus. Holy Mary, Mother of God, pray for us sinners, now and at the hour of our death. Amen.

Behold the handmaid of the Lord:

**R.** Be it done unto me according to thy word.

Hail Mary, full of grace, the Lord is with thee; blessed art thou among women and blessed is the fruit of thy womb, Jesus. Holy Mary, Mother of God, pray for us sinners, now and at the hour of our death. Amen.

And the word was made flesh:

**R.** And dwelt among us.

Hail Mary, full of grace, the Lord is with thee; blessed art thou among women and blessed is the fruit of thy womb, Jesus. Holy Mary, Mother of God, pray for us sinners, now and at the hour of our death. Amen.

**V.** Pray for us, O Holy Mother of God

**R.** That we may be made worthy of the promises of Christ.

*Let us pray:*

Pour forth, we beseech thee, O Lord, thy grace into our hearts; that we, to whom the incarnation of Christ, thy Son, was made known by the message of an angel, may by his passion and cross be brought to the glory of his resurrection, through the same Christ Our Lord.

Amen.

# SAINT LUIGI GONZAGA

## A LIFE OF EVANGELICAL PURITY

"May the example and intercession
of Saint Aloysius Gonzaga...spur you,
dear young people, to make the most of the
virtue of evangelical purity."

—POPE BENEDICT XVI,
GENERAL AUDIENCE, JUNE 22, 2011

**FEAST DAY:** JUNE 21

**PATRONAGE:** CHRISTIAN YOUTH, AIDS PATIENTS AND CAREGIVERS,
JESUIT NOVICES, YOUNG STUDENTS

**W**hile most English speakers know him as Aloysius Gonzaga, his family, friends, and much of the universal Church today have known him as Luigi. Born March 9, 1568, to Ferrante Gonzaga and his wife, Marta, his were far from humble beginnings. His military-minded father was an Italian marquis and prince of the Holy Roman Empire and his mother was a Spanish lady-in-waiting to the second wife of the Spanish King Philip II, Elisabeth of Valois. Thus, Luigi's upbringing was definitely not the norm for a Renaissance-era boy.

Baptized immediately after birth, Luigi had received a blessing from his mother in the form of a sign of the cross, but when he was born he didn't move and seemed to be dead. After an hour, he cried only a bit, motivating his mom to make a promise to Mary that she and her son, her first child, would make a pilgrimage to Loreto in thanksgiving if everything turned out OK. Marta, a woman of deep faith, had been spiritually preparing for her son long before he was born. After marrying Ferrante in 1566, she had moved to his castle in Castiglione, making fervent use of the personal chapel. She frequented Mass in the parish church and performed charitable deeds among the area peasants. On April 20, 1568, when Luigi was but a little over one and a half months old, he received the supplementary rite of baptism. Life was good—as his godfather was a duke, and to celebrate the baptism, his family gave out treasures and sweets throughout the town!

*"May he be happy, and live for ever, dear to God and men."*
*—Annotation in the Gonzaga family's parish registry,*
*April 20, 1568*

From the start, faith was important in the Gonzaga family. Luigi's mother taught him how to make the sign of the cross, to say the Our Father and Hail Mary, and the names of Jesus and Mary were some of his first words. She was also a model of almsgiving for her son, showing him what it meant to be a good steward of resources and giving him things to in turn practice charity himself. While Luigi's father was also a Catholic, he was not entirely happy with Luigi's strong spiritual inclinations from a young age, perhaps hoping he would eventually turn out more like his younger brother Ridolpho, who was energetic, loud, and in general a sharp contrast to the more introverted older son. As the first-born son, Luigi would eventually be the lord of Castiglione, taking on the vast majority of his father's wealth, titles, and responsibilities, and likely his father felt that it simply wouldn't do for him to enter into religious life.

When Luigi was three and Ridolpho was two, Ferrante decided that Luigi needed a tutor, feeling that he was already too easygoing and would need training for the military life he would undoubtedly lead as an Italian nobleman. On October 7, 1571, the battle of Lepanto was unleashed, and Ferrante was appointed to lead a defensive army of 3,000 men from Milan to Tunis, but he first would head to Casal, Italy. There he trained his troops for a month. Bringing four-year-old Luigi with him, he decked the child out in a mini-military outfit consisting of a suit of armor, lance, helmet, sword, belt, and even a holder for gunpowder! He encouraged the little boy to load a gun with gunpowder and fire it, but at one point the gunpowder backfired in his face, burning his skin. Explosives were off-limits to him after that. But even though he was being watched by his tutor, Don Pier Francesco del Turco, the young Luigi one day managed to sneak away while the soldiers were taking a nap.

> **Primogeniture:** The custom of a first-born child's inheritance of all or the vast majority of the titles/ property linked to an estate

He took some of a soldier's gunpowder and set off a cannon, making Ferrante think a soldier might be mutinying. By the time Ferrante was journeying to Tunis and Luigi went back to his home of Castiglione with del Turco, the boy had picked up the bad language of the military camp. His tutor warned him to cease using this language, especially when he got home to his mother.

> **Marta Gonzaga,** Luigi's mother, had offered him to God while visiting the Basilica della Santa Casa (Italy) when Luigi was an infant. She believed that Madonna della Santa Casa (Loreto) had taken care of him throughout his life.

It was then that he resolved to stop forever—a promise he seems to have kept. His mother believed that Madonna della Santa Casa (Loreto) had taken care of him throughout his life.

By 1574, Ferrante was back with his troops from Tunisia and immediately went to Spain for two years to serve under King Philip in Madrid. Meanwhile, Luigi was seven years old and continued to learn prayers by heart, including the Gradual and Penitential Psalms. He suffered from an illness for a year and a half, and around this time, his family—fearful of a plague around Castiglione—moved west to Monferrato.

When Luigi was nine, Ferrante, weary from gout, decided to get some relief from the baths in Lucca. He took Luigi and Ridolpho with him, planning to drop them off in Florence on his way back in order to gain some educational advantages with the grand duke. Their younger brother and sister, Carlo and Isabella, stayed with their mother, and the two older brothers lived in Florence with their tutor del Turco and an array of servants for two years, spending summers back in Castiglione. As young noblemen, the boys were constantly waited upon and always had guardians. Luigi was very obedient to authority figures and treated the servants with the utmost respect, perhaps stemming from his very mature belief that there is "no difference between the carcase of a prince and that of his servant." Luigi continued to be a stark contrast to Ridolpho, who was interested in athletics and the military. This young scholar divided his time between studying Latin, occasionally visiting the duke and other nobles, and playing sports when his tutor prodded him to do so, preferring personally spending quiet time by himself in conversation with God. Dedicated to

> **Gradual Psalms:** Psalms 119–133; probably called such because of their enormous popularity in being recited while walking to celebrate religious feasts.
>
> **Penitential Psalms:** Psalms 6, 32, 38, 51, 102, 130, and 143; especially prayed when examining one's conscience or asking for God's mercy and pardon.

> **Gout:** A disease where defective metabolism causes arthritis, and creates acute pain in small bones such as those in the feet

the development of his spiritual life, Luigi not only prayed regularly but worked hard to overcome emotions of anger. Upon going to confession for the first time, he felt so sorry for his sins that he passed out in front of his Jesuit confessor. At age ten, in the church of the Annunciation in Florence, young Luigi made a personal promise of chastity in front of the Mary statue. From then on, he made a special effort to keep custody of his eyes, making sure to be pure in his view of the world and its people.

In November 1579, Luigi was eleven years old when he and his brother moved to Mantua to be closer to their family in Castiglione. Living in a palace, Luigi had courtly life and parties constantly at his fingertips, but he disdained them. When he got sick soon after arriving, he was put on a rationed diet and allowed the opportunity to avoid courtly socializing to concentrate on schooling. This was a relief to Luigi, making him realize more than ever that he wanted to give his life to the Church.

**Saint Charles Borromeo, 1538–1584:** An Italian Counter-Reformer known for his involvement with the Council of Trent and encouragement of Catholic education

In the freedom of home at Castiglione, Luigi began praying for hours at a time before the crucifix. He challenged himself to say a Hail Mary when approaching a new flight of stairs and learned about meditation from a book by Father Peter Canisius, SJ. Venturing out from home, Luigi helped to catechize local children. In the summer of 1580, twelve-year-old Luigi had the opportunity to get to know Charles Cardinal

**Saint Peter Canisius, SJ, 1521–1597:** A Dutch Jesuit and doctor of the Church who helped lead the Counter-Reformation

Borromeo of Milan, who visited his family at Castiglione. Luigi received his first Communion from him and was encouraged to received Communion as often as he could.

 **One of Saint Charles Borromeo's** most famous gifts to the Church was the confessional booth; it was because of his own devotion to this sacrament that he came up with the idea of a miniature wooden room, where a penitent could confess his or her sins in relative anonymity behind a screen.

*When you go to confession, do you prefer to be behind a screen or face to face with a priest? Why?*

By the end of the summer, the family was reunited with Ferrante, as he had previously been occupied with business. Noticing his son's intense spiritual fervor, Ferrante tried to distract Luigi, who was continuing to avoid the normal pursuits of a nobleman. While athletics and games might be the normal things many pre-teen boys of the era enjoyed, Luigi preferred to speak with educated Catholic men about intellectual matters. He frequently spoke with local Benedictine and Dominican monks, went to nearby chapels, and read books about the lives of the saints. Such endeavors challenged his intellect, and he also fed his soul with regular fasting and prayers, spoken aloud and silently throughout his days. It was also around this time that he began to hint to his mother that he was feeling called to religious life. However, his family was distracted with the responsibilities of being a powerful, sixteenth-century noble family.

*"An extraordinary love of humility displayed itself in all his familiar words and sayings; frequently did he extol detachment from greatness and worldly dignities...Sometimes I accompanied him to the church, and, young as he was, he surpassed the oldest religious in acts of most humble devotion, in which he was as one perpetually weeping."*
—Dominican Father Claudio Fini

In 1581, the Gonzaga family was invited to stay at the Spanish court of King Philip II. Ferrante, Marta, Luigi, Ridolpho, their sister Isabella, and the family tutor accepted the invitation, while the three youngest siblings stayed at home. While Ferrante served as chamberlain, Luigi and Ridolpho were pages.

Luigi studied, keeping very busy with his page duties and academics, and found a Jesuit in Madrid—Father Fernando Paterno—to be his spiritual director. Forever involved in activity befitting a young nobleman, he enjoyed spending time in prayer and with sacred Scripture. He especially enjoyed mental prayer, finding an out-of-the-way closet where he could get some privacy and work to avoid distraction when in conversation

> **Chamberlain:** A title, sometimes purely honorary, signifying a household manager

with God. When Luigi began wearing patched, worn-out clothes, he made his father—who had new clothes made for him—upset, believing it improper behavior for a nobleman. Luigi even hid when other young noblemen would come to visit him, as he knew they would abhor his choice of

> **Mental prayer:** Silent contemplation of God

dress. By the end of 1582, after living in Madrid for about a year and a half, the Spanish prince, attended by this noble family, died.

*Have you ever known someone who was wealthy, but you didn't realize this fact when you first met the person?*

---

---

---

---

---

Around this time, Luigi began to openly share his call to religious life with his mother, Marta. While first considering the Franciscans in Spain or an order that was totally contemplative, the new Society of Jesus was very attractive to the teenager. Luigi liked that the Jesuits took an additional vow to obey the pope, spent time in teaching young people, and did foreign mission work. At about fifteen and a half years old, on the feast of the Assumption of Mary, Luigi prayed for Mary's guidance to discern his call and received a definite internal answer of "Yes."

He discussed the experience with his spiritual director and asked him to talk to his Jesuit superiors, but he was informed that the Jesuits would not take him without his parents' permission. He spoke to his mother that same day, and she was happy with his call. Knowing what Ferrante's attitude on the matter would likely be, she offered to speak with him herself.

Let's just say Ferrante didn't take the news very well. Incensed, when Luigi came to discuss the matter with him, he threatened to beat him and created a laundry list of people to blame for his son's vocational call, including his wife. He accused her of favoring Ridolpho and desiring to make him the sole inheritor of Ferrante's property. Furthermore, Ferrante blamed Luigi's spiritual director, since he was himself a Jesuit, but Luigi had never discussed his vocation with him before the feast of the Assumption. Ferrante also feared that because he was a gambling addict, this might be an elaborate family plot to get him to change his ways. Seeking a third party, he asked a Franciscan cousin to figure out if Luigi really had a calling. After a two-hour interview with the teenager, Ferrante's cousin believed that Luigi was indeed called. This became a stalemate, for when Ferrante delayed giving a response to his oldest son, Luigi took matters into his own hands. Going out for a walk with Ridolpho and their servants, they stopped by the Jesuits', and Lu-

**Feast of the Assumption of Mary:** The August 15 feast celebrates the end of Mary's earthly life and her assumption into heaven as queen.

igi told Ridolpho to head home while he intended to stay. As Ridolpho couldn't convince him to come back, Ferrante, who at the time was sick with gout, sent one of his assistants to the Jesuits to get him. Luigi wouldn't leave, so his father sent his assistant again, ordering Luigi to come home. Obediently, he did so.

*Have you or any of your friends been in a position where you've tried to pursue a spiritual activity, and your parents have reacted negatively?*

It was time for a compromise. Ferrante asked his same Franciscan cousin to talk Luigi out of joining the Jesuits, convincing him of the good he could do as a faithful nobleman. But the Franciscan refused, as he too was a former nobleman and once had been in the same awkward position as Luigi. However, everything seemed pretty much resolved when his father said that if he returned to Italy with the rest of the family, instead of joining the Society in Spain, he could do whatever he liked when he got back. Seventeen-year-old Luigi, who had been gone from Italy for three years, agreed, but when they had gotten back to Castiglione, his father delayed, wanting to distract his son by sending Luigi and Ridolpho on visits to various Italian princes' kingdoms to see more of the sort of life he could continue to live as a nobleman. Ridolpho was excited about the new clothes specially made for the trip, but Luigi refused to wear them. Continuing in his normal routine as much as possible by praying and fasting on the road, visiting various Jesuit houses, and even creating his own image of a cross if there wasn't one hanging in the room he was staying in. On one occasion, he reprimanded a seventy-year-old man who was speaking scandalously, saying, "How is it that an aged man of your lordship's quality is not ashamed to talk in this wise before all these young gentlemen? This is to give scandal and a bad example...."

That fall, Luigi returned to his family home and his father acted as if the promise he'd made was never solid. To complicate things, an Italian duke sent a bishop to let Luigi know that he would do more good as a nobleman priest who could rise in the ranks of the hierarchy than a Jesuit, who would not be able to own property or take on titles unless the pope ordered it. Furthermore, his Uncle Alfonso Gonzaga, whose daughter Caterina he was intended to marry, was none too happy. Various personalities were enticed to persuade young Gonzaga to enter another order, which included one Dominican who regretted being dragged into the matter and is recorded to have said, "I was sent to do the devil's work with that youth."

Finally, the seventeen-year-old's father gave in, but the struggle wasn't over. Luigi would have to formally renounce the title of marquis and go on behalf of his father to Milan on business. While there, he took classes in physics and math at the Jesuit college, and when he couldn't make it to class because business prevented him, he sent a servant to take notes. When his father again tried to convince him to abandon his plan to join the Jesuits, he turned the emotional level of this conflict up another notch, weeping and

> **Father General:** The leader of the Society of Jesus, also known as the Jesuits

claiming that Luigi's plan to join the Jesuits would kill him. Luigi wrote to the Jesuit Father General, asking that he be able to flee to a Jesuit

**Society of Jesus shield**

house before his father could do anything further. When he received a negative response, he tried to talk to Ferrante, who denied giving his approval, retorting that he wanted to wait to give his permission until Luigi was closer to twenty-five, as he would be firmer in his vocation, older, and healthier. He added that Luigi could do whatever he wanted, but he wouldn't have his blessing and would be cut off from the family. When Luigi said he would wait two or three years if his father would just agree to allow him to live in Rome to study, and write down their agreement to send it to the Jesuit Father General, Ferrante initially refused. His father held off for two more days before relenting and trying to insist that Luigi live with several servants, in the style of a nobleman.

This was too much for Luigi, who told him, "My lord and father, I place myself entirely in your hands; do with me what you will; but I

**Pope Sixtus V, (1520–1590):** Born into poverty, he became a Franciscan novice at the age of twelve and is known for his role in the Counter-Reformation.

protest to you that I am called by God to the company of Jesus, and that in resisting this call you resist the will of God." Luigi's words struck him, and, at long last, he released Luigi. With the estate's servants and peasants mourning his departure, and the inheritance renunciation finally official, everything was set for Luigi's entrance into the Society of Jesus. Ferrante, usually a generous man, refused to give him money for the Society to cover his needs while there. Luigi changed into an outfit he had had made that looked like Jesuit attire and traveled south to Rome for the novitiate. When Luigi's travel companion commented that Ridolpho must be joyful at the thought of taking over his inheritance, Luigi replied, "His joy at succeeding to it cannot equal mine in renouncing it." Visiting family and friends along the way, Luigi also stopped at the Holy House of Loreto, reaching Rome in late November 1585. He delivered the letter from his father to the Father General and received Pope Sixtus V's blessing on Saturday, November 23. On November 25, the feast of Saint Catherine, he entered the novitiate. From there he underwent a probationary period, spending time in a cell for silence and alone time.

**Saint Catherine of Alexandria:** A fourth-century saint, she is known to have won many people to the Christian faith while a teenager as a result of her debating skills.

During his two years as a novice at Saint Andrea Novitiate House, Luigi was known for his obedience and love of humble things. He traded his nicer clerical clothing and breviary for more common ones and took on the most menial tasks. His life was balanced among prayer, academic work, and physical labor which included helping the sick in hospitals and visiting prisons. As a novice, his spiritual life flourished. After an hour of mental prayer in the morning, he served five or six Masses and received Communion as often as possible, becoming known for his practiced ability to avoid distraction while at prayer.

Not long after his novitiate ended in October 1586, his novice master Father Pescatore got ill and was sent to Naples to recuperate. Three more sickly Jesuits were sent along with him, including Luigi, who was suffering from headaches. When they arrived on November 1 in Naples, Luigi studied metaphysics and was put in a bedroom with lots of others so his devotional practices would rub off on them. Unfortunately, they were not attentive to Luigi's health, as he wore a thin coat and paltry clothes and went without sheets while ill one night. Thus, by May 1587, he was sent back to Rome.

**After Luigi left,** his father became sicker with gout, stopped gambling, and more deeply regretted his past misdeeds. He went to confession and died February 13, 1586, three months after Luigi's renunciation of his titles and inheritance.

**Novice master:** The person whose task it is to educate religious who are in novitiate formation

# FAMILY DRAMA

*Just because Luigi was living as a Jesuit didn't mean that he was immune to the craziness that is part of being a member of any family. The difference between Luigi's family drama and your average Renaissance teen was that this was noble family drama. This meant that wars, disinheritances, and cousin-marrying were involved. Luigi's role in all of this was that he was typically the peacekeeper between various factions. When things got ridiculous, the family would call upon Luigi, at the time in his early twenties, to come and make amends. People trusted his opinion and valued his honest, clear thinking.*

*One such instance was when there was family turmoil over an inheritance of land that was supposed to go to Ridolpho. Troops*

**Saint Robert Bellarmine:** Italian Jesuit whose feast is September 17; was instrumental in the Counter-Reformation

*were at the ready to fight, and Luigi's mother, Marta, asked that he come and act as a diplomat between Ridolpho and the duke of Mantua. At first, he refused, but both Jesuit Father Robert Bellarmine and the Father General told him to go.*

*Luigi asked his traveling companion, a religious brother, that he never be left alone with his family while at home, as he was dedicated to his communal life. In his parents' household, he chose to live as he would at the Jesuit house, preferring to always walk instead of taking the horse or carriage a nobleman would have used, and refusing to be served by servants in day-to-day tasks such as making his own bed. He also kept up his devotional practices as usual, praying for three hours before bedtime. Finally, his cousin Vincenzo renounced the claim to Ridolpho's land, and there was peace for the Gonzagas.*

*Sadly, Luigi's services were needed again shortly thereafter. In the wake of Luigi's choice to disinherit himself, his brother, Ridolpho, was expected to marry his cousin, Caterina, the girl Luigi was originally supposed to marry, for land succession purposes. Ridolpho didn't seem to be in favor of his cousin and fell in love with another girl, Elena Aliprandi. She wasn't a noble, but she was good-looking and wealthy, so, with the permission of the bishop, he secretly married her in the presence of a priest and witnesses. Because his mother and older brother weren't made aware that they were married, but instead thought he was living in sin with Elena, Marta considered the relationship inappropriate and had Luigi try to convince him to marry his cousin Caterina. On November 25, 1589, Luigi met with Ridolpho in Milan, where he had promised to discuss the marriage to Caterina and explain everything. By the end of January 1590, his brother finally showed up and admitted he had been married to Elena for fifteen months. Luigi, happy that his brother wasn't being unchaste, got advice from other Jesuits and told Ridolpho he'd have to make his marriage public because making it seem like he and Elena were living in sin was causing a scandal. Luigi,*

**Scandal:** Modeling behavior that causes another to do evil.

*the family diplomat, told Ridolpho to either have Elena move out or admit that they were married. Ridolpho picked the latter plan and let Marta in on the secret himself, leaving his twenty-two-year-old big brother to break the news to the rest of the family, including Caterina.*

**After helping Ridolpho** with his marriage debacle, Luigi had spiritual advice that practically everyone should live by. He wrote him a letter urging him to:

1. Go to confession. "I recommend this very strongly to your lordship."
2. Pray every morning.
3. Do an examination of conscience before going to bed.
"...I would not have you lie down to rest at night before examining yourself as to whether you have offended God...."
4. Be respectful to your relatives.

On November 25, 1587 (the feast of Saint Catherine), after two years in novitiate with the Jesuits, Luigi made vows of poverty, chastity, and obedience. February and March of 1588 saw him having his head shaved, a tradition called tonsure, and receiving minor orders.

**From a letter** written December 11, 1587, to his mother:

"I announce to you the donation I made of myself to his Divine Majesty by taking my vows on Saint Catherine's day, for which, while inviting you, Signora, to praise the Lord, I at the same time beg you to beseech him that I may observe them, and advance in the state to which he has called me, so that, together, after this life is over, we may be united in the possession of him in heaven, where he is so lovingly expecting all his own. I accept at the same time the offer which you made me, Signora, in your last, of some more money for defraying the expenses of letters; I will beg you therefore to let me have twenty-five scudi. In conclusion, I recommend myself to you in the Lord, from whom I solicit for you increase of his holy grace in all things.

I am, illustrious Signora,
Your most obedient son in Christ,
Luigi Gonzaga, of the company of Jesus"

Over the next years, Luigi continued to increase in holiness and enjoyed time spent with lay brothers who were employed in humbler jobs. He would make an effort to sit with them at meals and refused to be treated as special because of his noble background and his weak health. Furthermore, Luigi would humbly beg in the streets and do the dirtiest of chores around the Jesuit house, including the removal of cobwebs, working in the kitchen, making beds and washing feet at the hospital. His humble day-to-day attitude accentuated for all the life of holiness of this young Jesuit. When anyone of importance was around, he would attempt to avoid notice by grabbing a broom and sweeping. Still, he was friendly to newcomers, specifically reaching out to them to discuss devout topics and encouraging his peers and elders alike to use recreation time to speak of holy things.

By November 1590, the young Jesuit had started his fourth year of theology, and, through prayer, had ascertained that he would not live a long life. When plague ravaged Italy, hitting Rome particularly hard the previous year, Luigi asked that he be able to serve the sick in the Jesuit hospital. As he was weak himself, his superiors were reluctant, but he persisted. On February 26, 1591, he wrote a letter to his brother, and by the next week, he was sick in bed. The sickness lasted for seven days, and when it seemed like Luigi was about to die, he went to confession and received anointing of the sick and Communion. It was his twenty-third birthday.

**Luigi** had a speech impediment that was noticeable when he said words with the letter "r."

Luigi continued to live, but fell so fatally ill that a false report that he had died was produced and sent to his family in Castiglione, where a funeral Mass was said for him. This was corrected in the next report sent to his home, but a letter from Luigi to his mother reveals his happy state of mind while his body was frail: "The doctors, who do not know what the result will be, are occupied in prescribing remedies for bodily health; for myself, however, it behooves me to think that God our Lord desires to bestow on me more perfect health than any the doctors can give, and so I pass my time joyfully, with the hope of being called, before many months are over, from the land of the dead to that of the living, and from the company of men here below to that of angels and saints in heaven...." The young man was so looking forward to spending eternity with God that he was frequently found during this period saying the *Te Deum*, as a prayer in thanksgiving to God.

*Te Deum* prayer of thanksgiving can be found on page 118

By June 1591, Luigi was not getting better, but he was still positive, consolingly telling his mother, "We shall not be long separated; we shall

**When he heard** that Luigi was mortally ill, the pope sent his blessing and a plenary indulgence to him.

meet again above and never more to part; we shall enjoy together a blissful union with our Redeemer, praising him with all our powers and eternally singing his mercies." For his last eight evenings, Luigi meditated each night on the Seven Penitential Psalms. Luigi insisted he would die, though the infirmarian kept saying he was better. Nearing the end, all 150 Jesuits gathered with Luigi when he next received Communion. Luigi hugged each of them, and died later the night of June 21, 1591, with the name of Jesus on his lips. He had been a Jesuit for six years.

After Luigi's death, his brother Jesuits found wounds in his side and knees calloused from kneeling. He was immediately considered a saint by those who lived with him, and after his body was processed to the Church, crowds of people tried to cut off different parts of his body: ear, finger, etc., and some succeeded! While it was normally the protocol for Jesuit bodies to just be laid in a grave, it was decided to put Luigi in a coffin. He was canonized December 31, 1726, by Pope Benedict XIII.

*"…I discovered in him such abundance of divine light, that I must confess that, at my advanced age, I learned from this youth how to meditate." —Saint Robert Bellarmine*

## Catechetical Connection: Contemplative Prayer

From a very young age, Saint Luigi practiced contemplative prayer. He didn't do it because it naturally came easily to him, as it is evidently something that he had to work very hard to achieve, but because his highest desire was closeness with God.

"What is contemplative prayer? Saint Teresa answers: 'Contemplative prayer [*oracion mental*] in my opinion is nothing else than a close sharing between friends; it means taking time frequently to be alone with him who we know loves us.' Contemplative prayer seeks him 'whom my soul loves.' It is Jesus, and in him, the Father. We seek him, because to desire him is always the beginning of love, and we seek him in that pure faith which causes us to be born of him and to live in him. In this inner prayer we can still meditate, but our attention is fixed on the Lord himself" (*CCC* 2709).

*How often do you take time for close sharing with the Lord?*

_____

_____

*What time of day is best for you to set aside for quiet time with God?*

_____

_____

# PRAYER TO SAINT LUIGI GONZAGA

*O holy Aloysius, beautiful for your angelic virtues,*
*I, your most unworthy client, recommend to you,*
*in a particular manner, the purity of my soul and body.*

*I beseech you, by your angelic chastity,*
*to recommend me to the Immaculate Lamb, Christ Jesus,*
*and to his most Holy Mother, the Virgin of Virgins,*
*and to preserve me from all sin.*

*Never permit me to be defiled by any stain of impurity,*
*but when you see me exposed to temptation*
*and the danger of sin,*
*remove far from my heart all impure thoughts and affections,*
*and, renewing in me the remembrance of eternity,*
*and of Jesus crucified,*
*imprint deeply in my soul the fear of God,*
*and enkindle within me the fire of divine love,*
*that, imitating you on earth, I may be worthy to have God*
*for my possession with you in heaven.*
*Amen.*

—*Adapted from Prayer to Saint Aloysius Gonzaga,*
*from Edward Healy Thompon's* The Life of Aloysius Gonzaga

# MEMORY VERSE

## PSALM 141:3

"Set a guard, LORD, before my mouth,
keep watch over the door of my lips."

*This was one of Luigi's very favorite psalms, so much so that he quoted it often. He was very careful regarding what he said and thought about, and tried very hard to be humble—taking correction without complaining.*

*How much control do you have over what you say?*

_____

_____

_____

_____

_____

*Which is more difficult for you to avoid: bad language, saying hurtfully critical things, or gossip? Write down a specific resolution to avoid one or more of those things.*

_____

_____

_____

_____

_____

# Saintly Challenges

- As a young child, Luigi memorized all the Gradual and Penitential Psalms. Choose one of the Gradual Psalms to know by heart.

- In a journal, copy the Penitential Psalm most close to your present spiritual disposition and express to God something you are sorry for.

- Make a plan to receive the sacrament of reconciliation.

- Luigi enjoyed helping catechize younger children.
  *Volunteer to help with Vacation Bible School or religious education at your parish.*

- As a young teenager deepening his spiritual focus, Luigi would pray on his knees, challenging himself to one hour of mental prayer a day, and if he lost focus, he would begin the hour again!
  *In our busy, noisy world, it is difficult to concentrate on one thing at a time. Pick something you enjoy that doesn't have to be plugged in, whether it is praying, biking, writing, drawing, reading, etc. Try focusing on that one thing for half an hour—forget multi-tasking, texting, or getting distracted, and enjoy that one pursuit.*
  *Was this difficult to do? Did you succeed? How long did you last? Do you think you could work your way up to an hour? Why or why not?*

- In his room, Luigi kept prints of Saint Catherine and Saint Thomas Aquinas to inspire him to holiness. Pick a saint or two who really inspires you, and print out a picture for your own room.

# THE TE DEUM

You are God: we praise you;
You are God: we acclaim you;
You are the eternal Father:
All creation worships you.
To you all angels, all the powers of heaven,
Cherubim and Seraphim, sing in endless praise:
Holy, holy, holy, Lord, God of power and might,
Heaven and earth are full of your glory.
The glorious company of apostles praise you.
The noble fellowship of prophets praise you.
The white-robed army of martyrs praise you.
Throughout the world the holy Church acclaims you:
Father, of majesty unbounded,
Your true and only Son, worthy of all worship,
And the Holy Spirit, advocate and guide.
You, Christ, are the king of glory,
The eternal Son of the Father.
When you became man to set us free
You did not spurn the Virgin's womb.
You overcame the sting of death,
And opened the kingdom of heaven to all believers.
You are seated at God's right hand in glory.
We believe that you will come, and be our judge.
Come then, Lord, and help your people,
Bought with the price of your own blood,
And bring us with your saints
To glory everlasting.
Save your people, Lord, and bless your inheritance.
Govern and uphold them now and always.
Day by day we bless you.
We praise your name forever.
Keep us today, Lord, from all sin.
Have mercy on us, Lord, have mercy.
Lord, show us your love and mercy;
For we put our trust in you.
In you, Lord, is our hope:
And we shall never hope in vain.

# SAINT ROSE OF VITERBO

# FAITHFUL AND GENEROUS TO THE POOR

"The young Saint Rose…is a shining example
of faith and generosity to the poor."

— POPE BENEDICT XVI, SEPTEMBER 6, 2009,
HOMILY DURING PASTORAL VISIT TO VITERBO AND BAGNOREGIO

**FEAST DAY:** SEPTEMBER 4

**PATRONAGE:** EXILES; THOSE REJECTED BY RELIGIOUS ORDERS;
VITERBO, ITALY

Though saints are born into households of various economic situations, Rose came from a family that struggled to make ends meet. We do not know their last name, but we do know that Rose's father and mother, John and Catherine, were older parents when Rose was born around the year 1233. They worked for the Poor Clares' convent in Viterbo, and the family lived in a small house attached to the nuns' monastery. Even though Rose's family did not have an abundance of material things, she was brought up by extremely devout people who were rich in faith.

**Poor Clares:** Contemplative order of Franciscan nuns founded by Clare of Assisi

*What has been your own experience with religious sisters? What orders have you gotten to know? Have you ever thought of volunteering to help them in their apostolate?*

Living practically side-by-side with the sisters, Rose was a very young child when she first started going to the church to pray. At the age of three years old it is recorded that her first miraculous occurrence took place. Her aunt had taken sick and died. After the body was put in a coffin, Rose joined her aunt's other family and friends in grieving. Full of faith, the little girl kneeled down, lifted her hands into the air, and prayed out loud, saying her aunt's name. Suddenly, the aunt became alert and fully alive, rising from the coffin and from the dead. It was not long after, around age seven, that Rose began to do little penances and seek out silence for contemplation.

Accounts vary as to her age, but when Rose was in her late tweens or early teens, Mary appeared to the girl while she was struggling with an illness. It turned out that the Virgin was asking her to become a Third Order Franciscan, calling Viterbo to penance and preaching against heresy afflicting the region. Additionally, she was to help bring the people back to obedience to the pope, as at that time, the Roman Emperor Frederick II was at odds with the Holy See. Rose followed through for the next couple of years, becoming a highly influential young force for the gospel in the city. Rose organized holy marches through the streets to preach the Good News, the central reason for her holy movement being the cross of Jesus. In the streets she lamented the ugliness of sin and amassed throngs of people to support her Christian message. In fact, the young roving preacher was so very effective in speaking out against the secular authorities and convincing people to be loyal to the pope, rather than Emperor Frederick II, that many began to take notice and get worried. Finally, in January 1250, the city's governor banished her family from Viterbo.

Due to the governor's decree, they were forced to seek shelter elsewhere, so they roamed to the neighboring city of Soriano. It was there, in early December 1250, that Rose predicted that Frederick II would die and his ill treatment of the papacy would end. On the thirteenth

**Pope Innocent IV:** Approved the Poor Clares' Rule; died in 1254

of that very same month, Rose's prediction came to fruition. Eventually they packed up again and headed for Vitorchiano (about eight miles away from Viterbo), where a sorceress was gaining renown. Determined to stand off against her and demonstrate the all-powerful authority of God, Rose managed to convert the town by resolutely standing in flames that did not burn her.

By 1251, Rose and her family were allowed to move back to Viterbo, as the town was once again being governed by Pope Innocent IV. Seeking to live out her vocation as a religious sister, Rose applied for entrance into the Saint Mary of the Roses convent, a place she had grown up next to and known well. Unfortunately, because her family was impoverished and she had no dowry to support her living expenses as a nun, she was not accepted into the congregation. However, Rose was not one to become discouraged and quit. She predicted she would eventually be allowed to live there and proceeded to live a solitary life in her parents' home, emulating the rhythms of religious life.

On March 6, 1252, Rose of Viterbo died at the age of seventeen, but her prediction that the monastery would finally accept her application amazingly still came true. Her body was eventually moved to the monastery five years later, on September 4, to be entombed at the convent where she'd been denied entrance. The cause for her canonization was opened up the same year she died and became official 200 years later, under the reign of Pope Callixtus III.

**Pope Callixtus III, 1378–1458**: Known for declaring the teenage martyr Saint Joan of Arc to be innocent of wrongdoing

# THE FEAST OF SAINT ROSE

Extraordinarily, Rose's body is incorrupt now, almost 800 years after her death. Rose's parents' humble little house has been turned into a chapel and a tomb fit for a saint. In this humble chapel, Rose lies clothed in the Poor Clare habit she never wore in life. Apparently, Saint Rose's scapular—a monastic garment worn over the head which drapes down, covering one's chest and back—miraculously kept French weapons from assaulting Viterbo. While the curtains shielding Saint Rose's body caught fire about 300 years ago, the body is unharmed, but it does appear a bit smoky.

> **Incorrupt:** Without decay or decomposition

To this day, Saint Rose's September 4 feast day is the single greatest celebration in the city of Viterbo. It is on this day that the curtain shielding her tomb is pulled away to reveal the still-incorrupt body. The celebration festivities go on for four days, with people coming in great numbers from all over to attend. Red banners hang from balconies, music plays in the streets, there is a raffle and horse racing, and the incredible Macchina of Saint Rose is processed through the town.

> **In addition to Rose's body,** the house holding her chapel and tomb also contains some cannonballs.

> **Macchina of Saint Rose:** An almost 100-foot tower built by the townspeople, it is covered until 8 p.m. on the evening of September 3, the night before the feast, when the lights (originally all candles) are lit by the local fire department. With a statue of Saint Rose at the top, the Macchina moves through the the streets of Viterbo carried by sixty people to commemorate the event of her body being moved from her family's parish church to the tomb at the Poor Clares' convent. Today, the Macchina carriers receive a special blessing beforehand, but it used to be, because of the tower's extreme weight and therefore danger, that it was required that one go to confession and receive Communion beforehand.

*Radiate*

## Catechetical Connection: Love for the Poor

Not only did Saint Rose of Viterbo preach to the poor, but she and her family were impoverished themselves. She preached unceasingly, giving of herself to the end.

> "'The Church's love for the poor...is a part of her constant tradition.' This love is inspired by the Gospel of the Beatitudes, of the poverty of Jesus, and of his concern for the poor. Love for the poor is even one of the motives for the duty of working so as to 'be able to give to those in need.' It extends not only to material poverty but also to the many forms of cultural and religious poverty" (*CCC* 2444).

**Saint Rose of Viterbo's** renown is as a lay Franciscan willing to preach the gospel whenever and wherever, despite persecution directed toward both herself and her family. From being booted from her hometown for allegiance to the pope to her inability to become a nun on account of her family's lack of material resources, her life is practically an unfolding of the Beatitudes.

### MATTHEW 5:3–12

**Blessed are the poor in spirit,** for theirs is the kingdom of heaven.

**Blessed are they who mourn,** for they will be comforted.

**Blessed are the meek,** for they will inherit the land.

**Blessed are they who hunger and thirst for righteousness,** for they will be satisfied.

**Blessed are the merciful,** for they will be shown mercy.

**Blessed are the clean of heart,** for they will see God.

**Blessed are the peacemakers,** for they will be called children of God.

**Blessed are they who are persecuted for the sake of righteousness,** for theirs is the kingdom of heaven.

**Blessed are you** when they insult you and persecute you and utter every kind of evil against you [falsely] because of me.

**Rejoice and be glad,** for your reward will be great in heaven. Thus they persecuted the prophets who were before you."

"Love for the poor is incompatible with immoderate love of riches or their selfish use" (*CCC* 2445).

*Is there anything you own that you love "immoderately"—more than you should care for it? If so, how did you develop such a strong attachment?*

*How do you care for people who are less materially fortunate than yourself?*

## PRAYER TO SAINT ROSE OF VITERBO

*Saint Rose of Viterbo,*
*From a young age, you opened yourself up*
*to the mystery of silence in order to hear the Lord's voice*
*and serve his people through preaching and holy poverty.*
*Aid me in answering the call to grow in unabashed sanctity,*
*serve your people's spiritual and material needs,*
*and live for you alone,*
*even when that makes me unpopular or ostracized.*
*Give me a heart for all your people,*
*especially those who are more difficult for me to love.*
*Amen.*

# MEMORY VERSE

## LUKE 7:14

"He stepped forward and touched the coffin;
at this the bearers halted, and he said,
'Young man, I tell you, arise!'"

*In Luke 7, the widow weeps over her dead son.*
*Have you ever grieved over the death of a loved one?*

It is most likely the case that very few of us will experience what it is like to see someone who has risen from the dead. However, when we participate in the sacrament of reconciliation, the deadness of sin is cast off and only that which is most alive and vital remains.

*Try to put into words what you feel like after receiving God's forgiveness in the sacrament of reconciliation.*

# Saintly Challenges

- Even today, money can be an impediment to a person's vocational calling—such as in the case of someone who has outstanding student loans. Fortunately, there are organizations springing up that work to help those who hear the call but have incurred debt.

  *Hold a fundraiser for the financial needs of seminarians' debts in either your own diocese or elsewhere.*

# SAINT PETER YU TAE-CHOL

## GLADLY DIED FOR THE SAKE OF CHRIST

"From the thirteen-year-old Peter Yu to the seventy-two-year-old Mark Chong, men and women, clergy and laity, rich and poor, ordinary people and nobles, many of them descendants of earlier unsung martyrs—they all gladly died for the sake of Christ."

—POPE JOHN PAUL II, MAY 6, 1984, MASS FOR THE
CANONIZATION OF KOREAN MARTYRS

**FEAST DAY:** SEPTEMBER 20

L ike many teenagers, Saint Peter Yu Tae-chol was born into a family where one parent practiced the Catholic faith and one did not. While he and Augustine, his father, were baptized Catholics, his mom and sister chose not to become Christians. Peter's mother discouraged her son's practice of Catholicism, encouraging him to make sacrificial offerings to their ancestors instead. While he was criticized for not obeying her, he refused to give worship to anyone but the Lord God, and otherwise tried to be an obedient son.

*Is there a particular family member or close friend who has encouraged you to grow and learn about your faith? If so, what in particular has the person done to make an impact on the way you live and worship?*

Young Peter very much looked up to his dad, an interpreter for the Korean government, especially when it came to matters such as principles and how to live morally. At the time that Augustine was initially learning about the Christian faith, there were no priests in Korea, which was also known as the "Hermit Kingdom." Starting in the late 1700s and continuing for 250 years, all outsiders except those from China had been excluded from the country. While

**Today,** forty-nine percent of the population of South Korea is Christian.

on a diplomatic trip to China, Augustine managed to secretly meet with the bishop there and be baptized. In 1826, the same year that his son Peter was born, he wrote a letter to the pope asking him to send missionary priests to Korea to evangelize and administer the sacraments. Due to this same letter, on September 9, 1831, Pope Gregory XVI established Korea as an official mission territory. Tragically, the first bishop of Korea died on his way there, and Augustine acted as a missionary in his own right.

In July 1839, when Peter was thirteen years old, persecution of Christians in Korea had dramatically increased. It was during this time of hostility that Augustine was found out to be a Catholic by his employer, the Korean government. As a result, he was arrested and accused of treason. While he was advised by family members to give up Christianity, he was steadfast and went a step further in refusing to inform the government of other Catholics. He is remembered as declaring, "Once having known God, I cannot possibly betray him," and he was rewarded for his grit with three bouts of torture over the six months that he was imprisoned.

With Augustine in mortal danger, Peter's mother and sister were concerned for Peter and thought he should deny his Lord. Instead, inspired by his father's fortitude, Peter bravely turned himself in to government officials, declaring himself a Catholic. While we have no way of knowing if Peter expected the torture that was to come, he surely knew that his path forward would not be an easy one. He was put in prison and encouraged to give up his faith. When harshly struck on the leg by a guard, Peter was asked if he believed in God. He rejoined courageously, stating that not only did he believe in God, but he wasn't afraid of being hit! On another occasion, when a guard told him he would force a hot coal in Peter's mouth, the teenager opened his mouth willingly, daring the guard to go ahead. While the guard didn't act on his words, Peter faced more abuse. At one juncture, he was assaulted to the point of unconsciousness. In all, he was questioned and tortured fourteen times, lashed 600 times, and clubbed forty-five times.

Though tough, his glad demeanor radiated throughout the ordeal; but this didn't exactly make him a avorite with his captors. His peace and happiness in the face of ridicule and abuse angered his guards, who must have seen his behavior as provoking them. After one particularly gruesome session of abuse, Peter smiled and picked off pieces of his own torn shoulder flesh, flinging them down to the ground in front of the judges. Two of the judges encouraged him to renounce his faith.

*Personality-wise, how do you tend to react when you are faced with a difficult situation?*

_____

_____

_____

_____

Not only did Peter withstand brutal treatment courageously, but he fortified and invigorated his fellow Catholics' spirits while in prison, urging apostates, those who had denied the faith out of fear, to come back to it. He is remembered as urging one individual on, saying, "You are a catechist and a grown man. I am only a boy; it is you who ought to be exhorting me to suffer courageously; how comes it that we have changed places? Return to yourself, and die for Jesus Christ."

*Is there someone in your life who could use some encouragement to live as a Christian? How can you help him/her to press on in the name of Christ?*

_____

_____

_____

_____

On September 22, 1839, Augustine's head was chopped off. Not long afterward, on October 31, 1839, thirteen-year-old Peter was sentenced to death and strangled in prison. Their daring martyrdom was far from being solely a father-son affair. Augustine and Peter were two of 10,000 martyrs to the Christian faith in Korea in the span of less than 100 years. Of those 10,000, he has the distinction of being the youngest of the 103 Catholic witnesses who were canonized by Blessed John Paul II in 1984.

> **By 1857,** there were 15,000 Catholics ministered to by seven priests in Korea, and by 1866, that number had increased to an amazing 23,000 Catholics and twelve priests.

# THE PRACTICE OF THE FAITH IN NORTH KOREA

In most Communist countries, transition of power can be a dramatic and bloody event. In North Korea, however, transition of power is dynastic—their current ruler is the son of the previous ruler, whose father was the man who founded the country. As a result, strict persecution of Christians that began with the country's founding continues to the present day. According to Aid to the Church in Need, about a quarter of North Korea's Christians are currently confined in labor camps, their crime being their Christian faith.

There are three Catholic dioceses in North Korea: Pyongyang, Hamhung, and Chunchon. All have been declared vacant by the Vatican, meaning that there are no Catholic bishops overseeing them. The Church still lists Francis Hong Yong-ho as bishop of Pyongyang, but he has been missing since 1962, and it's not known whether he's even alive. He joins the more than 300,000 North Korean Christians who have disappeared since 1953, their whereabouts unknown.

The atheistic government of North Korea goes to extraordinary lengths to shield its citizens from the message of Christianity. For example, in December 2011, it threatened South Korea with military action because of its decision to illuminate a Christmas tree-shaped tower within viewing distance of the North Korean border, calling it a form of "psychological warfare" on the part of the South. The United States Commission on International Religious Freedom perennially lists North Korea as one of the worst places in the world to be a Christian.

For more information on the state of Christianity in North Korea, visit Aid to the Church in Need at churchinneed.org.

## Catechetical Connection: Torture

Saint Peter Yu Tae-chol, along with many of the other 102 canonized Korean martyrs, encountered unspeakable tortures at the hands of those who wished to squelch the Christian faith. Unfortunately, torture is still committed toward Christians and non-Christians alike all over the world today. The catechism clearly speaks out against this disturbing practice.

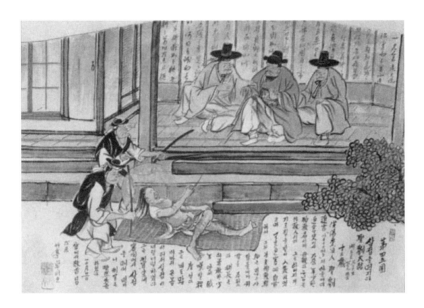

"Torture which uses physical or moral violence to extract confessions, punish the guilty, frighten opponents, or satisfy hatred is contrary to respect for the person and for human dignity. Except when performed for strictly therapeutic medical reasons, directly intended amputations, mutilations, and sterilizations performed on innocent persons are against the moral law" (*CCC* 2297).

*Hopefully you have never been around acts of torture, but chances are you have encountered bullying. Recall a time when you were the victim of a bully or exhibited bullying behavior yourself toward another person.*
*How did you feel afterward? If you were the victim, did you seek out help?*
*Have you forgiven the person(s) who bullied you? If you inflicted the bullying, did you seek forgiveness and make amends?*

# PRAYER OF AUGUSTINE YU CHIN-GIL, SAINT PETER YU TAE-CHOL'S FATHER

*"God, I thank you for the wonderful way*
*in which you have led me to baptism.*
*Send priests to our land so that the people there*
*who live in darkness*
*might have the joy of receiving the Eucharist.*
*May this foolish servant, no matter what suffering*
*or persecution is to come, give witness to you by offering my life in*
*the Lord's work of opening the eyes of our nation.*
*Give me the deep faith, strength, and courage that I need."*
*Amen.*

## MEMORY VERSE
### 2 CORINTHIANS 4:11

"For we who live are constantly being given up to
death for the sake of Jesus, so that the life of Jesus
may be manifested in our mortal flesh."

According to Blessed John Paul II at their canonization in Seoul, South Korea, "The Korean Martyrs have borne witness to the crucified and risen Christ. Through the sacrifice of their own lives they have become like Christ in a very special way. The words of Saint Paul the Apostle could truly have been spoken by them...The death of the martyrs is similar to the death of Christ on the cross, because like his, theirs has become the beginning of new life. This new life was manifested not only in themselves—in those who underwent death for Christ—but it was also extended to others. It became the leaven of the Church as the living community of disciples and witnesses to Jesus Christ. 'The blood of martyrs is the seed of Christians': this phrase from the first centuries of Christianity is confirmed before our eyes."

*How are martyrs' deaths like Christ's death on the cross?*

*How did you come to know of the Catholic faith? Was it passed on to you from relatives or friends?*

*Do you ever take your Christian faith for granted? If so, how?*

# Saintly Challenges

- Take some inspiration from Peter's father Augustine and write a letter to the pope!

  His Holiness, Pope _____
  Apostolic Palace
  00120 Vatican City

- Find out if there are any Masses said in Korean in your own diocese.

# ADDITIONAL MATERIALS

# Sources and Additional Permissions

Aelfric. *Life of Saint Lucy*. Trans. Walter W. Skeat, ed. University of Virginia. n.d. Web. May 29, 2012.

*Agnes beatae virginis*. Trans. Kathleen Pluth. Hymnography Unbound. 2010. Web.

Aronica, S.D.B., Paul. *Rose of the Andes*. Paterson, New Jersey: Salesiana Publishers. 1957.

Benedict XVI. General Audience. June 22, 2011.

Benedict XVI. Address to Teachers and Students of The Almo Collegio Capranica. January 20, 2012.

Benedict XVI. Eucharistic Concelebration. September 6, 2009.

Benedict XVI. Homily During Holy Mass for the Imposition of the Sacred Pallium on Metropolitan Archbishops. June 29, 2011.

Benedict XVI. Homily on the Occasion of the Agora of Italian Youth. September 2, 2007.

Benedict XVI. Papal Mass on the Solemnity of the Holy Apostles Peter and Paul. June 28, 2010.

Benedict XVI. Torchlight Procession Homily, Lourdes, France. September 13, 2008.

Benedict XVI. Vigil With Young People, Freiburg, Germany. September 25, 2011.

Bertone, Tarcisio. Beatification Mass of the Servant of God Zepherin Namuncurá. November 11, 2012.

*Catechism of the Catholic Church*. 2nd Ed. Libreria Editrice Vaticana, 1997.

"The Catholic Church in Korea." *New Catholic Encyclopedia*. Vol. 8. 2nd ed. Detroit: Gale, 2003. pp. 237–240.

Catholic News Agency. *Church in Peru Joins in Celebration of Beatification of Argentinian Indian*. November 12, 2007. Web. May 29, 2012.

*Compendium of the Catechism of the Catholic Church*. Libreria Editrice Vaticana, 2005

Hage, Hyacinth. *The Life of Blessed Gabriel of Our Lady of Sorrows*. Philadelphia: H.L. Kilner & Co. 1910. Google Book.

John Paul II. Address of John Paul II to the Bishops of Japan. March 31, 2001.

John Paul II. Address of the Holy Father to the New Ambassador of Chile to the Holy See. June 18, 2001.

John Paul II. Mass for the Canonization of Korean Martyrs. May 6, 1984.

McEachern, Patricia. *A Holy Life: The Writings of Saint Bernadette of Lourdes*. San Francisco: Ignatius Press. 2005. Print.

*New American Bible,* revised edition *(NABRE)*. USCCB. Web. May 27, 2012.

*The New Glories of the Catholic Church*. Trans. Fathers of the London Oratory. London: Richardson and Son. 1859. Google Book.

Pascucci, S.D.B., *Philip J. Zepherin, the Last Cura*. New Rochelle, New York: Salesian Missions. 2004. Print

"Saint Yu Chin-gil Augustine." Catholic Bishops' Conference of Korea. n.d. Web. May 29, 2012.

Tennyson, Alfred. *Poems*. London: C. Kegan Paul & Co. 1878. Google Book.

Thompson, Edward Healy, Ed. *The Life of Saint Aloysius Gonzaga of the Company of Jesus*. London: Burns & Oates. 1867. Google Book.

Yuki SJ, Diego R. *The Martyr's Hill Nagasaki*. 26 Martyrs Museum. 1993. Print.

Zenit. *Argentine Village Witnesses Beatification of Native*. November 24, 2007. Web. May 29, 2012.

# Additional Permissions

*Agnes beatae virginis* by Saint Ambrose is used by permission of the copyright holder and translator, Kathleen Pluth.

*A Holy Life: The Writings of Saint Bernadette of Lourdes* by Patricia McEachern. Copyright © 2005 Patricia McEachern. All rights reserved. Used by permission of Ignatius Press, San Francisco.

*Church in Peru Joins in Celebration of Beatification of Argentinian Indian* by Catholic News Agency. Copyright © 2007 Catholic News Agency. All rights reserved. Used by permission of Catholic News Agency, Englewood, Colorado.

Permission to use excerpts from the 1993 booklet *The Martyrs Hill Nagasaki* by Diego R. Yuki, SJ, granted by Twenty-Six Martyrs Museum of Nagasaki City, Japan.

*Zepherin, the Last Cura: A Brief Account of the Life of Zepherin Namuncurá* by Philip J. Pascucci. Copyright © 2004 Philip J. Pascucci. All rights reserved. Used by permission of Salesian Missions, New Rochelle, New York.

The English translation of the *Te Deum* is by the International Consultation on English Texts.

# APPENDIX

## STABAT MATER DOLOROSA

*Stabat mater dolorosa*
*juxta Crucem lacrimosa,*
*dum pendebat Filius.*
*Cujus animam gementem,*
*contristatam et dolentem*
*pertransivit gladius.*
*O quam tristis et afflicta*
*fuit illa benedicta,*
*mater Unigeniti!*
*Quae moerebat et dolebat,*
*pia Mater, dum videbat*
*nati poenas inclyti.*
*Quis est homo qui non fleret,*
*matrem Christi si videret*
*in tanto supplicio?*
*Quis non posset contristari*
*Christi Matrem contemplari*
*dolentem cum Filio?*
*Pro peccatis suae gentis*
*vidit Iesum in tormentis,*
*et flagellis subditum.*
*Vidit suum dulcem Natum*
*moriendo desolatum,*
*dum emisit spiritum.*
*Eja, Mater, fons amoris*
*me sentire vim doloris*
*fac, ut tecum lugeam.*
*Fac, ut ardeat cor meum*
*in amando Christum Deum*
*ut sibi complaceam.*

## AT THE CROSS, HER STATION KEEPING

At the Cross her station keeping,
stood the mournful Mother weeping,
close to her Son to the last.
Through her heart, His sorrow sharing,
all His bitter anguish bearing,
now at length the sword has passed.
O how sad and sore distressed
was that Mother, highly blest,
of the sole-begotten One.
Christ above in torment hangs,
she beneath beholds the pangs
of her dying glorious Son.
Is there one who would not weep,
whelmed in miseries so deep,
Christ's dear Mother to behold?
Can the human heart refrain
from partaking in her pain,
in that Mother's pain untold?
For the sins of His own nation,
She saw Jesus wracked with torment,
All with scourges rent:
She beheld her tender Child,
Saw Him hang in desolation,
Till His spirit forth He sent.
O thou Mother! fount of love!
Touch my spirit from above,
make my heart with thine accord:
Make me feel as thou hast felt;
make my soul to glow and melt
with the love of Christ my Lord.

| | |
|---|---|
| Sancta Mater, istud agas, | Holy Mother! pierce me through, |
| crucifixi fige plagas | in my heart each wound renew |
| cordi meo valide. | of my Savior crucified: |
| Tui Nati vulnerati, | Let me share with thee His pain, |
| tam dignati pro me pati, | who for all my sins was slain, |
| poenas mecum divide. | who for me in torments died. |
| Fac me tecum pie flere, | Let me mingle tears with thee, |
| crucifixo condolere, | mourning Him who mourned for me, |
| donec ego vixero. | all the days that I may live: |
| Juxta Crucem tecum stare, | By the Cross with thee to stay, |
| et me tibi sociare | there with thee to weep and pray, |
| in planctu desidero. | is all I ask of thee to give. |
| Virgo virginum praeclara, | Virgin of all virgins blest!, |
| mihi iam non sis amara, | Listen to my fond request: |
| fac me tecum plangere. | let me share thy grief divine; |
| Fac, ut portem Christi mortem, | Let me, to my latest breath, |
| passionis fac consortem, | in my body bear the death |
| et plagas recolere. | of that dying Son of thine. |
| Fac me plagis vulnerari, | Wounded with His every wound, |
| fac me Cruce inebriari, | steep my soul till it hath swooned, |
| et cruore Filii. | in His very Blood away; |
| Flammis ne urar succensus, | Be to me, O Virgin, nigh, |
| per te, Virgo, sim defensus | lest in flames I burn and die, |
| in die judicii. | in His awful Judgment Day. |
| Christe, cum sit hinc exire, | Christ, when Thou shalt call me hence, |
| da per Matrem me venire | by Thy Mother my defense, |
| ad palmam victoriae. | by Thy Cross my victory; |
| Quando corpus morietur, | While my body here decays, |
| fac, ut animae donetur | may my soul Thy goodness praise, |
| paradisi gloria. | Safe in Paradise with Thee. |
| Amen. | Amen. |

**Translation by Edward Caswall, *Lyra Catholica* (1849)**

# Litany of
# Our Lady of Seven Sorrows

*by Pope Pius VII*

**V.** Lord, have mercy on us

**R.** Christ, have mercy on us.

**V.** Lord, have mercy on us. Christ, hear us.

**R.** Christ, graciously hear us.

God, the Father of heaven, have mercy on us.
God the Son, Redeemer of the world, have mercy on us.
God the Holy Spirit, have mercy on us.
Holy Mary, Mother of God, pray for us.
Holy Virgin of virgins, pray for us.
Mother of the Crucified, [etc.]
Sorrowful Mother
Mournful Mother
Sighing Mother
Afflicted Mother
Foresaken Mother
Desolate Mother
Mother most sad
Mother set around with anguish
Mother overwhelmed by grief
Mother transfixed by a sword
Mother crucified in thy heart
Mother bereaved of thy Son
Sighing Dove
Mother of Dolors

Fount of tears

Sea of bitterness

Field of tribulation

Mass of suffering

Mirror of patience

Rock of constancy

Remedy in perplexity

Joy of the afflicted

Ark of the desolate

Refuge of the abandoned

Shiled of the oppressed

Conqueror of the incredulous

Solace of the wretched

Medicine of the sick

Help of the faint

Strength of the weak

Protectress of those who fight

Haven of the shipwrecked

Calmer of tempests

Companion of the sorrowful

Retreat of those who groan

Terror of the treacherous

Standard-bearer of the Martyrs

Treasure of the Faithful

Light of Confessors

Pearl of Virgins

Comfort of Widows

Joy of all Saints

Queen of thy Servants

Holy Mary, who alone art unexampled

**V.** Pray for us, most Sorrowful Virgin,

**R.** That we may be made worthy of the promises of Christ.

*Let us pray.*

O God, in whose Passion, according to the prophecy of Simeon, a sword of grief pierced through the most sweet soul of Thy glorious Blessed Virgin Mother Mary: grant that we, who celebrate the memory of her Seven Sorrows, may obtain the happy effect of Thy Passion, Who lives and reigns world without end. Amen.